MW00973308

CLIMBING OUT
of
UNEXPECTED
VALLEYS

CLIMBING OUT

of

UNEXPECTED VALLEYS

Death, Rescue, Romance, Deceit

JANET JOHNSON

XULON PRESS

Xulon Press
2301 Lucien Way #415
Maitland, FL 32751
407.339.4217
www.xulonpress.com

© 2023 by Janet Johnson

All rights reserved solely by the author. The author guarantees all
contents are original and do not infringe upon the legal rights of any
other person or work. No part of this book may be reproduced in any
form without the permission of the author.

Due to the changing nature of the Internet, if there are any web addresses,
links, or URLs included in this manuscript, these may have been altered
and may no longer be accessible. The views and opinions shared in this
book belong solely to the author and do not necessarily reflect those
of the publisher. The publisher therefore disclaims responsibility for the
views or opinions expressed within the work.

Unless otherwise indicated, Scripture quotations taken from the New
King Jim Version (NKJV). Copyright © 1982 by Thomas Nelson, Inc.
Used by permission. All rights reserved.

Scripture quotations taken from the Holy Bible, New Living Translation
(NLT). Copyright ©1996, 2004, 2007 by Tyndale House Foundation.
Used by permission of Tyndale House Publishers, Inc.

Scripture quotations taken from the Holy Bible, New International
Version (NIV). Copyright © 1973, 1978, 1984, 2011 by Biblica, Inc.™.
Used by permission. All rights reserved.

Scripture quotations taken from the Contemporary English Version
(CEV). Copyright © 1995 American Bible Society. Used by permission.
All rights reserved.

Paperback ISBN-13: 978-1-66287-957-9
Ebook ISBN-13: 978-1-66287-958-6

GOD HAS BLESSED me with a beautiful Christian family. My five children and their exceptional spouses have blessed me with my thirteen super-special grandchildren. *The best memories of my life include each of these outstanding individuals.*

Back row: Jeremy (oldest son) and wife, Mary Ann; Jordan (middle son) and wife, Casey, in front of him; Laura Beth (youngest child) and husband, Chris Durbin; Jonathan (youngest son) and wife, Whitney, in front of him; Virginia, wife of Justin (second son).

Middle row: Emma Grace (oldest granddaughter), Nana, Tyler (oldest grandson) Jeremy's children

Front cluster: Cayson, Piper, Kambell, Kruze, Kensi, Keenlyn, Kaglee, Paisley, Caylor, Cambree, Camden.

The "K" names belong to Jordan, the "C" names belong to Jonathan, and the "P" names belong to Laura Beth

To my family:

May God continue to guide and keep you in His care as you walk by His side. I love you very much and pray that you will draw closer to our Savior as you read Nana's book and learn from my experiences as well as my mistakes.

Love, Mom/Nana

THE FIRST VALLEY began like a bomb going off, and just when we thought we had picked up the pieces, it went off again!

COVID-19! Every part of our world was rocked by this mysterious virus that snuck up on us like a venomous snake. Confusion and uncertainty surrounded us like a thick fog. The news media, the politicians, and the medical field all had their opinions, and they usually all went in different directions. Our churches, schools, businesses, and families were locked down. There were shortages of supplies, and masked faces haunted empty aisles of the grocery stores. What were we to do and who knew the truth? My husband, David, and I prayed together and read scripture and found that as always, that's the source of real truth. Christ Jesus said, "And you shall know the truth, and the truth shall make you free" (John 8:32 NKJV).

We claimed that scripture and decided we would no longer live trapped and in fear of this virus. Scripture also says we are designed to work together, not alone. "Just as our bodies have many parts and each part has a special function, so it is with Christ's body. We are many parts of one body, and we all belong to each other" (Rom. 12:4–5 NLT). Community is God's design for us and his ways are always perfect.

We made the decision to free ourselves from isolation and venture out into the world again. We agreed that wherever we went, we would use caution, hand sanitizer, distancing, and masks. Believing that God created us to be together and to help those in need, we responded to requests for Billy Graham Rapid Response Team Chaplains to assist in crisis situations across the US. We deployed nine different times during 2021 for one to two weeks each time:

February: Lake Charles, Louisiana—hurricane
March: Nashville, Tennessee—flooding
April: Indianapolis, Indiana—Fed Ex Facility Mass Shooting
June: Bolivar County, Mississippi—flooding
July: Metro Detroit, Michigan—flooding
July: Dearborn, Michigan—flooding
August: Houma, Louisiana—hurricane
August: Haywood County, North Carolina—flooding
September: Collierville, Tennessee—Kroger Shooting

*David and Janet before
the pandemic*

*David being presented with an
ice cream sundae during a
chaplain deployment.*

Friends and family had shown some concern about us
traveling so much, but we felt God's leading and hand
of protection. The September deployment was our last
one for the year. Fall cleanup around our house and
preparations for the upcoming holidays kept us busy at
home. David and I both experienced East Tennessee fall
allergies, and living in the woods proved to irritate them
even more. By early December, we were both fighting
upper respiratory issues. David went to the doctor and
received a negative COVID test and some medication. We
were both coughing a lot and didn't seem to be making
much progress. On December 11, our daughter-in-law

next door tested positive for COVID, and then we did too. How could it be that we had traveled all over the US and then stayed at home and got this evil virus? As we began to reflect, we concluded that it must have been transmitted at his older sister's funeral earlier in December. One by one, family members began to fall to the wayside with COVID until a total of nine had tested positive.

Since it was a Saturday afternoon, we knew we wouldn't be able to get the help we needed until Monday morning. David and I both felt like wet dishrags and laid lifelessly in the bed with no appetite or energy to do anything other than to drag ourselves to the restroom. Early on Monday morning, we prepared to go to the hospital to get a monoclonal infusion. David sat down to put on his shoes and said, "I'm beginning to have trouble breathing. "The oximeter read eighty-five, so we went straight to the ER where they immediately put him on oxygen. We were placed in separate rooms and tested positive for COVID. I was sent home, but David was admitted. Even though we were both positive, they wouldn't let me stay. The nurse said, "That would be too many COVID germs for the staff to be exposed to."

Two days later, the doctor said David would probably be released the next day, but he would most likely have to go home on oxygen. That depressed David, and he said, "I don't want to be one of those little old men who drag around an oxygen machine." Our two middle sons took turns donning the gown, gloves, and mask provided by the hospital in order to spend the daily visiting hours with their dad. He was still able to have conversations with them, and it proved to be a precious, much-valued time for the boys to spend with their dad. Just when we were thinking David would be released, his oxygen levels dropped. Over the next of couple days they continued to drop to a level where he was no longer able to maintain an adequate oxygen supply. After a conference call with the doctor, David and I agreed that we didn't have any other option but for him to be admitted to ICU. Without adequate oxygen, the vital organs would be affected and eventually shut down. The doctor said ICU would be able to monitor him closer and administer other treatments such as "proning." Placing the sickest COVID patients on their stomachs had proved to be successful in allowing oxygen to more easily get to the lungs. The doctor wanted to try this proning procedure to see if it would improve David's oxygen level.

I continued to have the same calm and peaceful spirit that I had experienced ever since our ER visit. My sister, being an accountant for the hospital, was able to help me become the designated person for the ICU two-hour daily visits. My COVID symptoms had subsided, but I was existing in a weakened physical state and seemed to be operating like a robot. My first visit turned out to be the only time David and I had any conversation. It was two sentences separated by two hours. He said, "It makes me feel so good when you are here." Two hours later, he said, "I'm sorry."

During the next seven days, he lay in the ICU hooked up to the ventilator. I would visit and talk about whatever I could think of, and then I would read aloud out of the book of John in the New Living Translation. I read really loudly, partly because he couldn't wear his hearing aids and partly because I thought there might be someone else around who needed to hear God's Word.

On day seven of ICU, there was a word of encouragement from the nurse, "He's doing some better today!" Oh, would he rally? Would he use the strength of the Lord to come back to me? I woke up early the next morning, anxious to hear the progress made through the night. I called the nurse's station needing an update on his progress. I was told she was in the room with him and would call me. I waited restlessly for the next two hours. Finally, the phone rang, and it was the ICU doctor.

I said, "Oh, I'm so glad you've called. I'm feeling a little anxious this morning."

She coldly responded, "Why would you feel anxious?"

My reply was, "Well, my husband is in ICU on a ventilator, and I don't know how he's doing this morning!"

Matter of factly, she stated, "Well, he's not doing so well this morning. The vent had to be turned to maximum, and his kidneys are in distress."

In a panic, I asked, "What do I need to do?"

The doctor urged, "Get here sooner rather than later."

I raced to the hospital and was met in the lobby by the palliative care nurse. She was very compassionate but broke the news that they didn't expect him to live through the day. Was this real or was I dreaming? My next thought was that our children needed to see their dad. I asked what we could do and was told that four could go in. I told her that that wouldn't work because we have five children. I volunteered to stay in the lobby if they could all go in. Two of the boys had not been vaccinated and had to get a negative COVID test before they could go in, and our daughter had to travel three and a half hours.

After I suited up and was able to see his motionless, expressionless body moving up and down only by the force of the machine, I saw he didn't look like my David. Waves of grief and tears rolled over me. The nurse said they were doing everything possible to keep him alive until our family arrived. High doses of blood pressure medication and maximum air was sustaining his life. "Yea, though I walk through the valley of the shadow of death, I will fear no evil; for you are with me; your rod and your staff, they comfort me" (Ps. 23:4 NKJV) kept rolling through my head. One by one, they arrived and touched and talked to their dad. At last, our daughter arrived, and we were told to let the staff know when we were ready to turn off the machines. We said our goodbyes and played "Great is Thy Faithfulness" on a cell phone. Ten minutes later, he was pronounced dead. The two-week rollercoaster ride had come to an abrupt halt.

My message to friends and family:

> "It is with exceeding sorrow and at the same time glorious inexpressible joy that I share with you that David is in the arms of Jesus. He left this world at 4:55p.m. today. Thank you to all of you for walking through this valley with our family. You have prayed, supported, and comforted us. That's what a Christian family does! Thank you again for loving us."

Laura Beth and Janet saw this sunset as they entered the elevator immediately after David's death. It seemed that they could see him rising through the clouds on his way to heaven.

As the Scriptures say, "People are like grass; their beauty is like a flower in the field. The grass withers and the flower fades. But the word of the Lord remains forever. And that word is the Good News that was preached to you" (1 Pet. 1:24–25 NLT). My question here is for all of us: "Are we ready?"

Even though I walked through a fog immediately after his death and for the next month, I still had this peace within. It had to be the peace that the Bible talks about in Philippians 4:6–7 (NLT): "Don't worry about anything; instead, pray about everything. Tell God what you need and thank him for all he has done. Then you will experience

God's peace, which exceeds anything we can understand. His peace will guard your hearts and minds as you live in Christ Jesus." It is for certain that I had been living in a constant state of prayer, and God was holding me up. He sustained me through the writing of the obituary, selection of pictures for the slide show, three hundred–plus people who came through the receiving friend's line, the memorial service, complete with David's request of the Gaither's "I'm Looking for a City," the Celebration of Life and our delayed family Christmas celebration.

Caring, loving people would ask, "How are you? Well, I didn't know. I didn't know much of anything. The only way I could describe how I was is by saying I was numb, walking in a fog, and just putting one foot in front of the other. Half of me was gone! How could I function as half a person? We knew each other inside and out, and we had carried each other's joys and burdens together day after day and year after year. There was no need to ask what he thought about something or what he wanted to eat or where he wanted to go—I already knew. Now there was total silence morning, noon, and night. He wasn't there to eat with, study the Bible and pray with, to walk with or sleep with, or anything else! Again, how could I function as half a person?

My climb out of this valley began by responding to a Billy Graham Chaplain call to minister to people recovering from remnants of a hurricane. People close to me wondered if it was too soon for me to go. Truthfully, I had to admit I had some doubts as well, but I felt the Holy Spirit urging me on. After all, my only chaplain partner before this had been my husband. When I drove up to the basecamp, I met a new chaplain partner for the deployment who was also a widow. As we ministered to others, she ministered to me throughout the whole week. She unexpectedly walked through an afternoon of "widow's fog" with me. Yes, it's a real thing! As we sat in a parking lot eating our sack lunches, I tried unsuccessfully to unlock my phone. I had used the same code for a couple of years but all of a sudden, I couldn't remember what it was. After the phone completely locked up, we spent the rest of the afternoon going back and forth between the Apple store and the Verizon store. I was told that all they could do was wipe the phone clean. I told them that wouldn't work, I would be helpless without my contacts, pictures, and information stored in my phone. I prayed for the Lord to help me. I prayed for my mind to be refreshed. All of a sudden, I entered the correct code and the phone opened! I thanked and hugged the young man at the counter. He looked at me with astonishment and said, "You're welcome, but I didn't do anything!"

What a blessing those seven days turned out to be. Some of the numbness and "widow's fog" was leaving, and healing had begun. By keeping my eyes off of myself and focusing on the Lord, I was able to see those suffering around me.

I was able to see we all have valleys to climb out of and I could climb right along beside others. "The generous will prosper; those who refresh others will themselves be refreshed (Prov. 11:25 NLT).

Upon returning home, I received a call from the Billy Graham headquarters asking how I held up during the deployment. I thanked the coordinator for placing me with a widow and shared how helpful it had been. She replied, "I didn't know she was a widow when I put you together!" There was God again! If He wasn't carrying me or walking by my side, He was at least one step ahead of me.

I responded to a second deployment in March for recovery from an ice storm in Memphis. Let me just say "ditto" to the paragraph above! I was placed with a different partner who had been a widow for seven years. She has continued to reach out to me for over a year.

An army of people stepped up to support me. My immediate family of twenty-four as well as our extended family supported me through the grief journey. What a lifeline they were for this stubbornly self-sufficient, independent woman. They walked with me and put up with my "I'm okay attitude" every step of the way. Doesn't the mama bear have to be the strongest and the bravest? Well, I must say that even mama bears need lots of support when they lose papa bear!

David and I had started a small group at our church a few years back. We had studied and prayed together, laughed, and cried together and shared one another's burdens. Little did David know how valuable these people would be to me after he left. They fed me physically and spiritually, sent me weekly cards, called, texted, and visited. They have truly been there for me. So many other people reached out to support me. Former students, neighbors, friends, church family, and even strangers. Every single person that was there for me propped me up just a little bit more. What a blessing it was to have all of these people. Unfortunately, it didn't change the fact that David wasn't here, and that he would not be coming back.

Not only was I dealing with grief, but so were my grown children and grandchildren. It doesn't really matter how old you are when you lose a parent or grandparent, it's still a shock and a huge adjustment. Even little five-year-old Cayson playing in the snow in my backyard almost a year later told me, "Grandad just threw a snowball from heaven at me!" Of course, that tore my heart out.

My family kept closer tabs on me and included me in their plans. This helped with my emotional state, but I still struggled with loneliness. I still struggled with my identity and what life was supposed to look like. Each time the family gathered at my home, the pain seemed a little less. We all still missed him so very much, but we were each dealing with it in our own ways. Some said they thought about him every day, some said they had picked up their phone to call and tell him something, and some just went about their day thinking quietly to themselves. Sometimes I wondered if I was any support for them. I have always tried to fix things and make life easier for my children, but this was just something I couldn't fix.

Each of my children have written some thoughts about life with their dad.

Laura Beth posted on Facebook:

Oh, my sweet daddy . . . my sounding board, encourager, and the first man I ever loved. You were the epitome of a good and faithful servant. You've left such an amazing legacy and touched so many lives. Thank you for showing us how to love as Jesus did. I know you're up there rejoicing and singing with the angels . . . and probably beating some old friends in Scrabble. We'll be missing you until we meet someday in heaven.

Love, Laura Beth.

Justin also posted on Facebook:

> I delayed writing this due to the lack of adequate words that would truly express what an impact our father made during his life. Whatever I say here will not give justice to what he accomplished on this earth. He was always teaching, helping, coaching, encouraging, and loving others. He definitely loved God, loved people, and served both. I never saw him lash out at or lay a hand on anyone in anger. He treated everybody the same and was always even, steady, and he was our earthly rock. If you were privileged to know him, he probably made an impact on your life in a positive way. He lived life abundantly, loved like Christ, and laughed daily. He will be mourned by many, missed by all who knew him, but never forgotten. Go rest high on that mountain; your work on earth is done.
>
> If you knew David Johnson, please leave a comment on how he affected your life, whether memory or story, a song he sang to you, or a nickname he called you. We want to read it even if he straightened out your hind end in school. I'm sure there are many that would bring us a smile.

And many former students responded with stories and comments.

The day of the Memorial Service for David, the pastor asked of any of the family wanted to say anything, and I said I didn't think so, but I would ask. Each one said "No" until I got to Jordan, and he said to my surprise that he had something to say. Boy, did he ever! I wasn't prepared for what he had to say.

"Your dad was my favorite teacher." I can't tell you how many times I have heard that! A lot of the time, people just come up to me out in town to tell me that. But I have wondered why. Why was he your favorite teacher? Did you just like PE class? Or was it because he made the PE class the most memorable PE class you had ever taken? Possibly, it was that he knew how to create a fun competition, but also made sure everyone felt part of a team. In some way, it felt like the students gave their best effort because they didn't want to let Dad down.

Or possibly your favorite subject was Tennessee history. Most likely, that was because he had the rare ability to teach in a way that brought history to life. He would tell the stories as if he had first-hand knowledge and would keep you on the edge of your seat. His students were learning our state's history without even realizing it. Was he your favorite teacher because of his personality? He loved making sure everyone was treated fairly and kindly, while pushing you to be your best. Most likely he gave you a nickname, and a good chance that nickname was sung to you from an oldie's song that you may have never even heard. Those songs were usually well timed and brought joy to a student that needed it. He always made his students feel like they had someone that cared for them. Even if he saw that student many years later, he would still greet them with "their" song.

Well, it turns out my dad was also my favorite teacher. For all the reasons that were just mentioned and so many more. Not only was he my favorite teacher in school, but outside the classroom as well. The list would be countless of the things he taught me—from shooting a basketball or riding a bike to making a fire and learning how to write a check. But on the other hand, a lot of times, Dad would teach through his actions. He taught me how to love a wife and treat her like a queen. I often noticed how he would grab my mom, swing her around, and give her a kiss, just because. He taught me with his actions how to be an amazing father: how to love your kids and have a special relationship with each child.

He taught me the importance of quality time with family. Whether it was playing scrabble, laughing over movie quotes, or just watching a game, we did it together. Whether it was at the beach, mountains, or in his living room, he just wanted to be with his family. He always showed us how to treat others, the way you would want to be treated. Most importantly, he taught me and my siblings the importance of having a personal relationship with Jesus Christ. He taught us the truth of who Jesus was and what He did for us. He led our family with laughter and joy that only came from the Lord. He was a true ambassador for Christ.

The last thing my dad taught me was in the final days of his life. I had the privilege of being by his side while in the hospital. That is where he taught me that no matter where we are or how we feel, that is our mission field. If we are willing to be used by God in any circumstance, He can use us. He showed that to me by making sure every nurse that walked into his room had a personal relationship with Jesus Christ, and most of the time, it led into a conversation about their faith.

He didn't want to pass up an opportunity to share the gospel. It was a powerful testimony to watch and a special time I had with him. I will never forget those last days and the final education he gave me. I am so thankful for all the lessons I learned from my dad and hope I can honor him by doing the same for my kids. My dad was my favorite teacher.

I didn't want to leave out the other two sons, so I asked them to write some thoughts about their dad. This is what Jonathan wrote:

When I think of my dad, I think of a godly man. Growing up, when I would wake up in the mornings, he had a Bible in his hand. When I would go to bed, he was studying the Word. He was a gentle and kind man, slow to anger, and he never raised his voice. I would go to him for advice on any situation. I think of him every day. I think of the lives he impacted as a father and as a teacher and friend. He was a selfless man and always put others first. He supported his children in everything we wanted to do and was always there for us. He enjoyed watching us play all types of sports and continued that tradition watching his grandchildren. My kids loved seeing their grandad cheering them on at their games.

He had a way of making others feel special and valued. To know him was to love him, and his fun-loving spirit was contagious to all those around him. He loved music, games, French fries, traveling, serving, fellowshipping, the beach, talking to everyone in town (we could rarely go anywhere without him seeing someone he knew and talking to them). He loved being connected to everyone. He loved our huge family and always enjoyed getting together with the whole Johnson clan every year. He lived his life for the Lord, led his family well, led others to Christ and encouraged us to do the same. His example lives on in me and in everyone he influenced. We will carry his memory and his legacy with us forever until we meet in heaven.

Jeremy wrote:

My dad influenced me in so many ways. He was a kind, generous, thoughtful, and loving man. Above all, he loved God and his family. I learned early on that the path I needed to be on was the one that leads to God. He portrayed his Christian values throughout his life and strived daily to be a servant of God and others. He was a teacher not only in school, but in the way he lived his life.

He encouraged and supported me in everything that I did.

Many lives were touched by my dad. He always wanted to talk with anyone who would talk to him. Stranger or not, it didn't matter. Whatever the circumstance, he made people feel comfortable and welcome. He was a fun-loving person, full of life, and had a smile that would light up a room. This is the person the rest of us need to be more like. Love God, love people—isn't that what we are called to do? Well, he lived it, and everyone around him experienced his love. Yes, we miss him down here on earth, but heaven gained another saint. Thank you, Dad for teaching me. Love you!

Our family would never be the same, but it was our goal to find a new normal. A friend shared this statement with me: Grief is not a place to stay but a place to journey through. "You, Lord God, are my fortress, that mighty rock where I am safe" (Ps. 94:22–23 CEV). I could not let myself or my family stay in the valley; we had to climb out!

"The Lord himself goes before you and will be with you; he will never leave you nor forsake you. Do not be afraid; do not be discouraged" (Deut. 31:8 NIV).

THE SECOND VALLEY started out as a calm, slow descent, and then I quickly crashed and hit bottom!

In April, I received a card in the mail that said I had a package available to be picked up at the local post office. I waited my turn in line at the post office and then handed the card to the lady at the window. A few minutes later, she returned with a box that was clearly printed "CREMATION REMAINS" over and over all around the box. I could feel eyes staring at me, from the people in line to everyone behind the counter. I calmly looked at her and said, "My husband is in this box!" and turned and walked out the door. When I got to the car, I sat in the parking lot and began to shake and cry uncontrollably. My brain was racing.

I needed someone to share this grief with, someone to physically be there for me. I called my sister-in-law, but she was on a road trip. I called my oldest son, Jeremy, and he didn't answer. My daughter, Laura Beth, was too far away, and my other sons were at work. Finally, I was able to reach my youngest son, Jonathan, and tell him what had happened. He was so precious and gentle and listened as I blubbered over the phone. No one had come to my side but eventually I was able to drive home. My next problem was that I couldn't bring myself to lift the box out of the car. It stayed there and rode around with me for the next two weeks until Justin was at the house. I told him I needed him to bring his dad in out of the car, that I just couldn't bring myself to do it. He asked where he should put him and my reply was, "In the closet!" Then I was in the valley again trying to decide what to do with a box of ashes that I couldn't bring myself to touch, much less open.

The church cemetery where we had installed a marker had informed us that any ashes left there would need to be in a crushproof container. That just didn't feel right to me. Next, I thought about how much he had loved the beach; I could take him to the ocean! I liked that idea. Then my mind went to the three wonderful years we had lived in Alaska. We had often reflected on those years and agreed that those years had been a life highlight for us. That was it! I would plan a trip and take some of his ashes to Alaska.

When my daughter's father-in-law, Chris, heard I was planning a trip to Alaska, he volunteered to go with me. His wife had passed away four months before David. Since he was recently retired, he would be able to return to places he had previously visited with her. They had taken a land/sea cruise during the time David and I had been living in Ketchikan. When they disembarked, we toured the town together, and then I whipped up some fresh salmon sandwiches for lunch. He still says to this day that it was the best he'd ever eaten.

We planned our trip for the last two weeks of June 2022. After all, if you travel that far you need to stay a while and see as much as possible. I didn't know where we would sprinkle the ashes, and I just kept praying and asking God to give me the right place. As we were hanging around Anchorage one Saturday, hitting the flea markets, we passed a Denali truck. David had purchased a truck just like that one about a year before he died. My mind wandered back to the day in November, a month before his passing, when he had told me he thought he ought to sell that truck. He said it was just too big, and he didn't really need it, so we took off to the dealership to see what they might give us. To our surprise they bought it back for five hundred dollars less than what he had paid for it! How many times have I reflected on that event and praised the Lord because that was one less major thing I had to deal with after David was gone. The Lord definitely went before us in the selling of the truck.

So that was it! The Denali truck led my thoughts to Denali Mountain! On Tuesday, we took off for the mountain, with ashes in a plastic water bottle. As we headed up Denali, the sky clouded over, and it began to rain. It was actually the only day during our entire trip that it rained. At mile fifteen, we followed a narrow pathway dotted with yellow and purple wildflowers. The only sound we could hear was the rain on our hoods and the rushing waters of the Savage River. At just the perfect spot, I kneeled down on the bank, opened the bottle and slowly let the ashes drift down the river. With tears running down my cheeks, we made our way back down the sweet little pathway. To my surprise, the rain stopped, and the sun broke through the clouds. My tears stopped, and I felt like I had just received a kiss from heaven. The trek back up the other side of "the valley" had begun.

> "Light is sweet, and it pleases the eyes to see the sun. However, many years anyone may live, let them enjoy them all" (Eccles. 11:7 NIV).

Denali, the highest peak in North America

A gray day at Savage River.

On the one-year anniversary of David's death, I went with my oldest son, Jeremy, to the gravesite. It was the first time I had been back to the cemetery since we had gathered as an extended family on April sixteenth, four months after his death. I hadn't been able to get all of the ashes in the water bottle that I took to Alaska so I decided to take some to sprinkle around the marker in the cemetery. They blended right into the patches of snow on the ground. David loved snow so that seemed an appropriate scenario. It was a sweet but tearful time. We read the words on the marker, looked for other family member's headstones, and reminiscently gazed at the beautiful mountain range in the background.

*Rose petals scattered by grandkids on
Grandad's marker in April 2021*

There were still ashes left! Where should I take the remaining ashes? I had already decided to take some to the beach, any beach. Then I relived the days that ran into weeks that we had spent creating a trail through the woods at our home. It was a quiet, peaceful place to walk on the acreage God had so graciously led us to purchase forty-nine years ago. It was where we had raised our family. Yes, right here at home would be the perfect place to leave the remaining ashes. I chuckled to myself as I imagined judgment day. I almost could hear David saying, "I would have been here sooner if you hadn't spread me out in so many different places!"

"And he will send out his angels with the mighty blast of a trumpet, and they will gather his chosen ones from all over the world—from the farthest ends of the earth and heaven" (Matt. 24:31 NLT). There will be no more emotional valleys there! What a glorious day that will be!

[The Lord says,] "Even to your old age and gray hairs, I am he, I am he who will sustain you. I have made you and I will carry you; I will sustain you and I will rescue you" (Isa. 46:4 NIV).

IT WAS A long way to the top of the next mountain, but the valley came way faster than I would have ever dreamed! After taking my husband's ashes to Denali National Park and spreading them in the Savage River, my traveling companion had a mission to accomplish. Several years back, his son-in-law had visited Anchorage, Alaska, and went with some buddies to hike Flattop Mountain. He told his father-in-law he didn't make it to the summit. So, we headed to Flattop with a goal of making it just a little bit further than his son-in-law.

These sixty-five and seventy-one-year-olds headed up the trail and had no intention of going to the top. We were huffing a little, but we took our time and passed the designated point. Chris commented, "If our kids could see us now, they would say we are crazy." We were making it okay even though we scrambled over and around huge rocks and formed our own trail straight up the mountain for the last 900 feet. We agreed, "We can't turn back now!" Yes, we made it to the summit at 3,510-foot elevation and had our picture taken holding onto the American flag. We were so proud as we took in the 360-degree view of glaciers, mountaintops, and valleys, with the city of Anchorage barely visible in the background.

Nearing the summit of Flattop Mountain

Janet and her friend, Chris, on top of Flattop Mountain

As we descended the summit, we quickly realized the way down was much more challenging. We slowly found our footing. At last, we were on nearly flat ground when my companion slipped on the scree. Arms and legs bloody and his body a little rattled, he cleaned up, and we headed on. Then I slipped. As if in slow motion, I sat down as my right foot slipped out in front of me. The problem was that my left foot was planted and turned behind me. After I heard a pop, I brought my leg around and knew my ankle was broken.

I tried to stand holding onto Chris, but I couldn't put any weight on my foot. Then I prayed out loud and said, "Dear Lord Jesus, I can't get off of this mountain! You will need to help me." It may have been a minute later when I heard a male voice say, "Ma'am, do you need help?" I said, "I sure do!" As he looked me in the eye, he confidently responded, "All four of us are paramedics, and three of us are firefighters. We know how to take care of you." I was absolutely amazed when God answered my prayer almost before I got it out of my mouth! Chris was a witness to it all and has given testimony to that fact!

Why was I amazed at how the Lord answered my prayer? After all, His Word says: "The righteous person faces many troubles, but the Lord comes to the rescue each time." Righteous? Was I righteous? Much of my life I have tried to live right with God, and I knew that I was His child, but I have sinned daily. Therefore, this righteousness His Word speaks of has to be a wonderful gift that is given to those who believe Jesus is God's Son and claim Him as their Savior. He sees His children as righteous!

Quickly, my ankle was wrapped in an ace bandage that they just "happened "to have in their pack. One called for assistance but was told that there were no responders available for that area, but a helicopter could be dispatched to a pick-up point. The paramedics said they could get me off the mountain if I didn't want the helicopter. When I recovered from lightheadedness, I told them I didn't want a helicopter and that I was ready to give it everything I had to get back to the parking lot. I began to scoot down the railroad-tie steps as they held my leg steady.

When roughly one hundred steps came to an end, they reevaluated our approach.

Stage 1 of the rescue

Plan B was the implementation of a two-man carry. With a rescuer on each side of me, I hopped on my good leg until the path narrowed. The rest of the two-and-a-half-mile trek was accomplished by the four rotating and carrying me piggyback to the parking lot. After our two-hour journey, I told them they were just like my four sons who were just too far away to rescue me! These four guys on the first day of their vacation from Mentor, Ohio, were the angels Jesus sent to rescue me. I will forever be grateful for their kindness, gentleness, and willingness to help a stranger.

The Rescuers

The story of my rescue traveled across the US and to several foreign countries as friends heard the story and then shared it with others. It was even aired on the Cleveland, Ohio, news. At the conclusion of the segment, the anchor looked at the camera and said, "That gives me goosebumps!" God received the glory, and He showed His ways to the nations.

BE STRONG! BE brave! Do not be afraid! Do not be discouraged! For the Lord your God will be with you wherever you go! (Wording based on Joshua 1:9)

After the fall, I would be in the valley for a while. The valley walls were steep and slippery, but I would not be discouraged. When the firefighters placed me in the front seat of our rental truck, I looked at the four of them and said, "I wish I had something to give you." One of them replied, "That's not necessary; this is just what we do." After a tender hug from each one, we headed off to the urgent care. They sent us to a second place that wound up sending us to a "walk-in" orthopedic clinic. I thought that to be rather funny since there was no way I would be walking in!

After a wheelchair was located, we went up to check in. Oddly enough, I was the only patient in the waiting room, and as soon as my paperwork was completed, they whisked me away to x-ray.

When completed, the technician commented, "Well, I can tell you, you're not faking it!" I replied, "Well, I could have told you that before you took the x-rays!" Next a little round doctor with a white beard, who reminded me of Santa Claus, came in and repeated over and over, "I'm just so sorry." Finally, I looked him in the eye and said, "I am too, but what are we going to do about it?" He said I needed surgery to which I replied, "I can't do that here. I have to go home." He conferred with a colleague and agreed to apply a cast from my toes to my knee to stabilize the three broken bones until I could get to Knoxville.

The tech started to wrap my leg and then stopped to ask me if I was fond of the pants I had worn that day. Yes, I told her, they were my travel pants. She helped me replace them with a huge pair of black paper shorts that I wrapped up under my legs to hold down the very wide legs. As the cast grew larger and larger, I commented that I wasn't going to be able to get on any of my pants. She said that I would probably need to go shopping. How was I to do that with a pair of paper shorts, a cast, and crutches I could hardly use? Besides, I was with a man who wasn't my husband! Oh, how I needed and missed David!

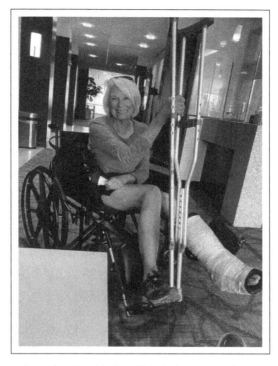

Janet leaving Alaska clinic in her paper shorts

We picked up pain meds at the Walgreens pharmacy (another blessing was Walgreens being the preferred pharmacy for my insurance). Upon trying to exit the truck at the Airbnb, I fell right on my behind because the weight of the cast threw me off balance. By the time I scooted up the steps, the tech who had applied my cast appeared at the door. She handed me a gift bag with two new pairs of capri pants that would fit over the cast! That was just another one of the God moments that would happen on my way back across the US.

Immediately, Chris and I began to search for flights back home. We were able to book a red-eye for that evening, but we only had two hours to clean up the house, pack our things, and race to return the rental vehicle. All of that was on Chris because I couldn't do anything to help. Upon arriving at the airport, I was placed in a wheelchair and pushed through security. Fortunately, they only made me stand long enough to run the wand up and down my cast and across my back. The attendant made sure I got safely to our gate. A transfer chair was used to wheel me backward down the aisle to a row with an extra seat that the airline graciously provided. That was a blessing too. The lady in front of us turned around and asked if she could pray for me. She laid her hand gently on my cast and asked God to carry me safely home and for excellent healing.

We made it to Chicago where I endured a six-hour layover. Chris would be flying from there to Kentucky, so he got me a smoothie and left me in my wheelchair, holding a pair of crutches, my purse, and a carry on! I made it okay for a while as curious onlookers asked about my situation. Each conversation provided me with the opportunity to witness how God had rescued me. Eventually, the inevitable happened. I had to go to the restroom. With all my belongings piled on my lap, I slowly started to roll toward the restroom. Progress halted when I had to negotiate a ramp! A traveler came up behind me and said, "Madam, I don't know what I'm going to do with my bag, but I'm going to push you." A lady walked up beside him and said, "You push her, and I'll get your bag." When we reached the restroom, an airport employee said, "I'll take her from here." Then she proceeded to tell me that she had been struck by a car and had been in a wheelchair the entire previous year. She assisted me and then took me back to the boarding area. I was reminded of Philippians 4:19 NIV that says, "And my God will meet all your needs according to the riches of his glory in Christ Jesus."

On the final leg of my flight, I was seated next to a thirty-four-year-old young man. We had a wonderful conversation the whole way home. Upon landing, knowing I would be the last one to be wheeled off, I told him, "I think you can just step over me." He replied, "No, I'm not leaving you. I'm going to get your bags." And he did just that. Plus, he waited with me until I begged him to go. I told him my sons were there to take me home. Again, God was faithful to supply all my needs.

The report from the Knoxville surgeon the next day was that my ankle was too swollen to do surgery. Two weeks later, my brother-in-law and sister-in-law took me for surgery. Even though I was very grateful for their help, that really hit me like a ton of bricks because my husband had been the only one to provide for me that way in the past. The surgery was successful, and I went home that day with a plate, eight screws, and another cast up to my knee. My sister was scheduled to spend the night with me. I reminded her of the times when we were growing up, and I had to pinch her to keep her on her side of the bed! Unexpectedly, my daughter and two granddaughters came that evening from Kentucky to be with me for a few days. Even though I was elated to see them, I was just a tad bit disappointed I didn't get to pinch my sister that night!

My house quickly became one with revolving doors as friends, neighbors, and family took care of my every need during the eight weeks I was in a wheelchair, two weeks on a walker, and one on a cane. After a month of therapy, life began to look more normal. I could walk again, and I was so very thankful.

As I've said before, I'm a strong, independent woman, and even though I didn't get discouraged, God humbled me during this process. He gave me time to be still and listen, time to grieve, and an extra portion of time in His Word and prayer. He also gave me time to notice just how much I'm loved. Sadly, I wasn't loved by my husband anymore, and I greatly missed that love. Humbled, I had to let go and let others show me God's love.

"For whoever exalts himself will be humbled, and whoever humbles himself will be exalted" (Matt. 23:12 NLT). The climb back up out of this valley had almost been accomplished.

"You alone are God! You make my feet run as fast as those of a deer, and you help me stand on the mountains" (Ps. 18:31, 33).

SEARCHING FOR A passage out of the valley of grief, I was mired in the mud, when suddenly I found myself on a mountaintop for just a little while.

David and I would have celebrated our fiftieth wedding anniversary on November third. That day was another one of "the firsts" after his passing. You know, the first missed birthday (his and mine), the first missed Christmas and Thanksgiving, the missed vacations, and each and every missed breakfast, lunch, and dinner. I took myself out to lunch that day and reminisced favorite anniversary celebrations. A very special one was when my daughter orchestrated a surprise party for our fortieth anniversary. I never dreamed then that we wouldn't make it to a fiftieth celebration. I'm so thankful now for the remembrance of that time with friends and family.

After my not-so-special anniversary lunch, I returned home and sat in the office reeling in sadness. I just kept thinking about how lonely I felt as each day since his death passed. I was surrounded by family, neighbors, and church family, so I did have people! I stayed active in the garden, lawn care, the church, community, and family. Why did I feel so lonely?

I had become accustomed to having the love of my life beside me all day every day. With both of us retired, we were able to come and go as we pleased. We could take a walk or take a drive. We could go to ballgames or play with grandkids. Life was good. In a two-week period of time, my whole world changed when David's life was no more. I missed having him to talk to, to pray with, and to love. I missed having him tell me I looked beautiful, kiss me, and hold me close. Reality hit when I acknowledged he would never be coming home.

Wallowing in sorrow, I began to wonder how I could meet someone in my area to share time with, someone who was walking through the same pain. Then maybe I wouldn't feel so lonely. I began to search on the internet for a singles Bible study in Maryville and then in Knoxville. I didn't find what I was looking for. I remembered how my son and daughter-in-law met on Christian Mingle and wondered if I could find someone close by that I could share a meal with occasionally. When I googled the site,

Match.com came up. I thought maybe I could peruse some profiles for free, but it showed that I needed to sign up. Reluctantly I put in my information and paid for a month. The answer to the first profile question (How do you start your day?) was coffee, Bible, and prayer. The description of what I was looking for in a relationship went something like this: "I'm looking for a Christian man to share everyday life with. To be there and support each other during good times and bad. I want someone who is passionate about sharing the gospel and is a strong Christian leader." I also indicated that alcohol, smoking, and drugs were deal breakers and that I was looking for someone within twenty-five miles.

The second day I was on the site, I began to receive "likes." I would read the profiles and disregard if they were too far away. If someone were really interested in exploring more, they would send a "match." That response went into a different category. On day three, I had received a couple of matches and began to dialogue with both of them, even though "Jim" was actually in Fayetteville, North Carolina. I also noticed on his profile that he was sixty-four.

In the next communication with "Jim," I pointed out both of those things. He replied that he wasn't tied to North Carolina and was willing to relocate. He also said that age didn't matter, but the heart did. I still wasn't all that interested in him and didn't really even like his pictures.

He wasn't smiling in any of the pictures, and I asked him if he ever smiled. He said of course he did, so I requested he send a "smiling photo."

The messages from Jim on the Match.com site were coming more and more frequently. (Jim is not the name used on the site.) It felt good to have someone care about what I was doing, where I was going, and so forth. He began to say more and more endearing things and asked more and more questions about my life. Then he asked if he could have my phone number so we could text and talk off the site. That was Mistake Number 1!

On November 9, he began texting and calling. I'm sharing this experience because it might protect someone else from starting down this slippery slope. Watch how he drew me in and connected to my heart. Look for the endearing terms he uses and how he flattered me. See how naively I shared my life details with him. Notice, too, how he used prayer and scripture to meet my desire to connect with a godly man.

Wednesday, November 9, 9:00 a.m.

Jim introduced himself on the text message and asked if I was having a good day. I replied and then asked if he was still employed. He said that he was still employed and planning to retire soon. Jim said he was a geologist with a degree in petroleum engineering and specialized in designing and developing methods for oil and gas extraction. He had worked for several companies in the past, such as Chevron Refinery, Pascagoula, Mississippi; Exxon Mobil Refinery, Theodore, Alabama; British Petroleum and Gas Processing (BP), offshore operations. He explained that he had retired from working for companies and became an independent contractor in order to take care of his sick wife. Of course, the fact that he had sacrificed to take care of his wife touched my heart.

I told Jim I had retired from education after thirty-eight years and as the children's director at my church for five years. My husband and I were enjoying retirement days together. We were traveling and spending time with family and grandkids; we had built a house and were just truly enjoying each other and life together. Then the Lord called my dear husband home and left me with emptiness. I thought it would be helpful to have someone to spend time with, who had experienced the same kind of loss. I had been searching the web for a local singles Bibles study group when I wound up on the Match.com site.

I told Jim that I was actually a little leery of the whole online process and that I hadn't told anyone about my decision to sign up. He responded that our happiness is a priority and that I had made the right decision because God didn't create us to be alone. He stated right away that he was interested in a long-term relationship. I explained to him that I might not be ready for that since it hadn't been quite a year since my husband had passed. I didn't know how my family would feel about that, and I wouldn't want to hurt them in any way. It was time to take care of grandchildren so I had to leave.

Wednesday, Nov 9, 8:07 p.m.

We had our first phone conversation. Jim told me that he thought I was beautiful, that he loved my smile, and that I didn't look my age at all. I noticed right away that he had an accent, and I said, "It sounds like you are from Kenya!" My travels had taken me to Kenya nine times, so I was very familiar with the accent. Why didn't I pursue that thought? Jim replied that he was born and raised in Germany and that English was his second language. This was missed clue No. 1.

Wed, November 9, 9:52 p.m. after phone call

Jim sent a text with kisses and hugs. He said he felt so happy talking to me and that I had a good laugh. He wished me a good night, and that was the end of day one off the dating site.

Thursday, November 10, 6:30 a.m.

Jim sent an early text saying that God has given us another day filled with more blessings than we could count. The routine daily text of "Good morning, I hope you rested well!" began on this day. I responded with "Good morning! His mercies are new each morning." Fall is absolutely my favorite time of year—the changing leaves, the cool crisp air, and the fog rising up through the mountains." He said that I brought a smile to his face, and he was looking forward to talking to me again. He wanted to know where my happy place was in my house. I told him that the office where I sit to read my Bible each morning was my favorite spot. I asked him if he was a US citizen, and he said yes and asked if I wanted to see his passport! I thought that was a weird response. He eventually ended the conversation by telling me I was gorgeous.

Thursday, November 10, 10:30 a.m.

Jim wanted to know what kind of music I liked because he wanted to share his favorite songs with me. I shared that I enjoyed a variety of music from Handel's Messiah, '60s hits, Southern Gospel, and hymns, to contemporary Christian music. Jim indicated he liked modern pop as well as favorite Christian musicians like Chris Tomlin, Lecrae, Toby Mac, and Lauren. Little did I know that the love songs he would share with me would have such an emotional effect.

Then he asked me what I would consider a deal breaker in a relationship. My response was smoking heavy drinking, immorality, and the lack of a relationship with Jesus. He said he wanted to go to church with me and that smoking, drugs, abuse, anger issues, poor hygiene, and dishonesty were deal breakers for him. He felt so lucky to have found someone like me. I said, "Let's take it a step at a time." I felt like he was moving too fast, so I kept my answers short and tried to keep an arm's length away. I tried to let him drive the conversation. Jim responded that one step at a time was what he wanted, too, and apologized if he was moving too fast. Missed clue No. 2 was that he was definitely moving too fast!

I headed outside to clean windows before the rain came.

Thursday, November 10, 12:30 p.m.

Jim asked if I had lunch, what my favorite foods were, and whether I liked to cook. I told him I did like to cook but that I had lost my motivation to cook when David died. I responded that I could eat about anything, but that in the winter I liked to fix a big pot of soup and eat on it for days. Steak, chicken, baked potatoes, sweet potatoes, and dessert were at the top of the list too. He said he liked to cook but that he missed doing that with a partner. He had a long list of favorite foods, but since he had "German roots," he liked stroganoff and bratwurst. Really?

Thursday, November 10, 4:00 p.m.

Jim texted that he was finished with work for the day and wondered if I was finished with the windows. He said he wished he could help me. Now, that sounded nice! Someone to work alongside of me.

Next, he wanted to know my favorite Bible verses. I told him there were too many to count but that Joshua 1:9 was the verse I had the grandkids memorize for Camp Johnson this year. I told him I was working on memorizing 1 Peter, chapter one. Jim indicated that he was impressed that I was having the kids memorize scripture. He said one of his favorites was "When God's people are in need, be ready to help them. Always be eager to practice hospitality" (Rom. 12:13 NLT). "Give your burdens to the Lord, and he will take care of you. He will not permit the godly to slip and fall" (Ps. 55:22 NLT). Was he using the words of scripture to plant seeds in my thoughts?

Thursday, November 10, 7:38 p.m.

Jim sent a text, and I didn't answer because I was at my grandson's basketball game. He asked if I was busy and wondered if we weren't going to talk on the phone before bed. I called him when I got home, but it went to voicemail. Missed red flag—Jim *never answered* any of my calls. He always returned my calls.

Thursday, November 10, 9:19 p.m.

After the phone call, he sent a link to Shania Twain's "From This Moment On" and said he was praying that angels would surround me as I slept. "Good night, my love" closed that day and most of the days following.

Friday, November 11, 7:46 a.m.

As I opened my eyes, I was greeted with Jim saying that he saw me the way God intended for him to see me, "in His own image and likeness." He told me I was an exquisite creature and a lovely being.

I responded, "Oh, that's beautiful! You seem to be a loving, caring, gentle man. You do know God's Word. May He bless you today." Jim said that it was a good feeling to wake up with me on his mind.

We chatted back and forth, and then he told me he would be setting up his Skype account after work so we could do a video call. I had asked him during the previous phone call if we could FaceTime, and he had given me some lame excuse about not being able to do that because of an issue with Android to iPhone. That made no sense to me, but I didn't make a big deal out of it. Now I know I should have.

Friday, November 11, 9:30 a.m.

Jim texted and asked what I liked to read. I responded that I liked to read the Bible. He laughed and said he knew that was what I would say. He liked to read the Bible and other books as well. One of his favorite books was *Death Angel* by Linda Howard. That sounded like a dark book to me. I asked him if he was at work, and he said he was preparing for a meeting where he would bid for gas and oil contracts. This was the point where the plot thickened!

Friday, November 11, 5:05 p.m.

We both set up Skype on our phones. We had difficulty connecting, so I suggested we use What's App or Messenger, and he said no, Skype would be better. Now I know that it was only because he was using someone else's video from a Facebook account. Anyway, when we did connect, it was poor quality and didn't last but a few minutes. Hummm! Why didn't I keep pursuing another method? Another red flag missed.

Friday, November 11, 7:00 p.m.

This day he started the conversation asking about my favorite color, when my birthday was, what kind of ice cream I liked and so forth. Then he asked if I had ever read the first five love languages by Gary Chapman? What man just comes out of the blue to talk about love languages? I told him we had a class at church about the love languages. Then he asked for my love language, listed in order of importance to me. This was my answer: No. 1. Words of affirmation; No. 2. Acts of service; No. 3. Quality time; No. 4. Touch; No. 5. Gifts. Jim responded with: No. 1. Quality time; No. 2. Physical touch; No. 3. Words of affirmation; No. 4. Acts of service; No. 5. Gifts.

Then he said he would like to know one of my favorite childhood memories. I responded with "Seeing the ocean for the first time when I was fifteen. You?" Jim said his favorite memory from childhood was learning from his grandmother how to knit woolen clothes.

Saturday, November 12, 8:32 a.m.

The first message of the day from Jim read something like this: You are alive this beautiful morning because of the amazing love of God and His tender mercies. In this brand-new day, may your steps be directed into the right places and may all the rough ways in your path be made smooth. Good morning, blessed one. Kisses and hugs! I was touched by this and told him how amazing he was and what a wonderful way to start my day. Jim responded that God had brought me to his path! He wanted to know if I had breakfast and coffee. I told him I had and that I had already read my Bible and prayed. He asked if I had prayed for him and for us. I told him I was praying for wisdom, discernment, and guidance in all things. He said, yes, that was the right prayer and that he had prayed the same thing and that he could hear the Holy Spirit telling him I was the one.

When I told him I didn't know what to say to that, he responded that I didn't have to say anything but that he had never met anyone like me. I told him it had only been a few days and that it concerned me that I hadn't met him in person, but I also said, "I'm not there yet!" Jim said that he hoped I would get there.

Sunday, Nov 13, 8:05 a.m.

Jim started out the day with another quote about life and how the day would be another opportunity to demand what we wanted and then see life sprinting toward us. I asked him if these things just flowed out of his brain, and he said they did, that he was great at writing poems. Many times, though, I could google his statements and see that they weren't original. I thought he was just trying to impress me.

Sunday, November 13, 12:07 p.m.

Jim texted that he missed me and wished I would realize how special I was to him. I said, "I think you should save that until you see my wrinkles and flab and the horns on my head! Can we plan to meet somewhere? I don't think I can move forward without actually being able to look you in the eyes!"

Sunday, November 13, 4:51 p.m.

Jim responded that he didn't want me to worry about that because beauty is in the eyes of the beholder. All he wanted was the beauty of the heart, and he wasn't a man interested only in physical appearance. He said he had a big week coming up with his project interview, but we could plan to meet somewhere afterward. I was nervous about meeting him. I suggested the little town of Black Mountain, North Carolina. It's a quaint little town with shops and cafés. That would have been a two-hour drive for me and five and a half for Jim. I was trying to be cautious by meeting in a public place and having my own vehicle for escape if needed.

Monday, November 14, 11:36 a.m.

Jim sent a photo of the board room with his notebook and name plate, bottle of water, and microphone. Interviewers were seated at a long, cloth-covered table in the background. I asked Jim if he was nervous, and he said he was. I told him I would pray for him.

Monday, November 14, 7:00 p.m.

Jim called to tell me he had good news about his interview and that he had gotten a confirmation email saying the contract was awarded to him. This was a big deal, something he had been praying about for a year. He gave God all the glory. It would be a twenty-one-day contract with specific deadlines. He would be the supervisor over fifteen men working on a platform located in the Gulf of Mexico. They would compete the task of locating drilling sites, extracting oil, and storing it in an oil rig. I congratulated him and told him I was happy to see he was giving God the glory. He said he was to report to the rig in forty-eight hours. This was another clue that I missed. This seemed to be an abnormally short amount of preparation time, but I didn't question it. Also, we were planning an in-person meeting. This was convenient timing on his part to avoid that. Jim said he believed everything happens for a reason and that he would never stop communicating with me. He said his feelings were growing stronger for me each day. I didn't express any feelings for him, but I was disappointed that he would be gone and we wouldn't be able to meet.

I received a text from Jim that was actually addressed to a Mr. Bryan. He said he was sending a copy of his driver's license for identification purposes. This was a decoy to reassure me it was a real project. I didn't get the undercurrent, though. I let him know he had sent the text to me instead of Mr. Bryan.

Tuesday, November 15, 7:11 a.m.

Jim's morning text said that I was alive that beautiful morning because of the tender mercy and amazing love of God. I responded, "Good morning to you! I wondered if you slept because you were exhausted or if you were awake because you were excited!" He said he was awake because he had a lot to accomplish. Jim said he had already gotten the mobilization fee from BP that morning. He thanked me for asking about details of the trip and called me "his love." He said he got goosebumps when he received messages from me because I was so sweet and caring.

Tuesday, November 15, 4:23 p.m.

Jim started the next text by asking if I was still on Match. com. I told him I hadn't cancelled it yet but that I had responded to a questionnaire that very day. They asked for a response to how I liked the site. I responded that they advertised as a Christian site, but most men on there are not interested in Christian women. He said that he had canceled his days ago and that he wanted me to cancel mine. (This was a lie because Jim appeared on Match after this statement.) He said he was happy that I had joined because if I hadn't, he would not have come across a wonderful soul like me. The fact that he wanted me off the site should have alerted me!

But instead, I told him I thought he was too good to be true. He wondered why I would say that, and I said, "Because you say all the right things! You're handsome, strong, smart, a poet, you love Jesus, and you're an independent contractor who just won a bid!" My vision had changed and I had grown to love his appearance. He thanked me for the compliment and said he was just a human being created by God. He told me he was fallible in nature and that no man is perfect. He said I was blessed because I was beautiful and had lovely children and grandkids, my love of Jesus, the fact that I lived in a house and had retired from a good job. I agreed with him. Jim said he wanted me to know that even though we had never met, he trusted me and that his instincts never fail him.

I asked if his parents were still living and if he had siblings. He said his parents were both deceased and that as an only child, his childhood was boring. The last time he had heard from his only living relative, his aunt, was after his mother passed away. It just made me feel so sad that this man had no one. His parents and his wife had passed away, and he didn't even have children. I felt so blessed to have three siblings and a large family.

Tuesday, November 15, 7:04 p.m.

Jim reported that he had confirmed his flight departure for Thursday 16:40 from Raleigh-Durham International airport to Houston. He would then fly from Houston to Merida (Mexican airport). After that, they would take a chopper from Merida to the platform in Gulf of Mexico. He texted that he just wanted to let me know: "I pray that the eyes of your heart may be enlightened in order that you may know the hope to which he has called you, the riches of his glorious inheritance in his holy people, and his incomparably great power for us who believe. That power is the same as his mighty strength." I responded that I couldn't remember where that passage was located. He said Ephesians 1:18–20 (NIV).

We talked on the phone before bed.

Wednesday, November 16, 5:59 a.m.

I awoke to this verse from Jim: "Praise be to the LORD for He has heard my cry for mercy. The LORD is my strength and my shield; my heart trusts in him, and he helps me. My heart leaps for joy, and with my song l praise him" (Ps. 28:6–7 NIV,) and "God is our refuge and strength, an ever-present help in trouble. Therefore, we will not fear, though the earth give way and the mountains fall into the heart of the sea, though its waters roar and foam and the mountains quake with their surging" (Ps. 46:1–3 NIV). He added, "But those who hope in the LORD will renew their strength. They will soar on wings like eagles; they will run and not grow weary, they will walk and not be faint" (Isa. 40:31 NIV). I responded that those were beautiful scriptures and the perfect way to start our day.

Wednesday, November 16, 1:58 p.m.

Jim texted that when he thought about me and our rich conversations, he felt a warmness inside. He said we had a special, amazing connection and that sometimes it made him feel like his heart would burst. He said all the longing and excitement made him feel that we were destined to be together but that it was just going to take a little longer than we had planned. He said that I was his best friend. I told him I thought it was crazy how this was happening and that I hoped it was genuine and not just a fantasy! I told him I didn't think we'd know for sure until we could look each other in the eye! Jim questioned why I thought it could be a fantasy and why I couldn't just trust in "us." He said he believed in "us." I told him I felt excited but that I just wanted to see him and know that he was real! I was having a hard time believing all of this was real. Jim responded by saying that I was beautiful and adorable, the type of woman he had prayed for God to bring into his life. He said that his prayers had been answered.

Thursday, November 17, 6:30 a.m.

Jim texted that he had opened his eyes with me on his mind. He called from the "airport" and prayed God would watch over me. Then he sent a selfie in his seat on the plane. I didn't hear from him again that day.

Friday, November 18, 5:45 a.m.

I was greeted with morning scriptures: "Love is patient and kind. It does not envy, it does not boast, it is not proud. It does not dishonor others, it is not self-seeking, it is not easily angered, it keeps no record of wrongs. Love does not delight in evil but rejoices with the truth. It always protects, always trusts, always hopes, always perseveres" (1 Cor. 13:4–7).

Jim said he looked at my pictures every day and smiled. He said he and the crew arrived to the platform safely and that he couldn't stop thinking about me! He said love hurts when we feel unable to help, when we feel powerless in the face of the pain of a loved one, in the face of the suffering of the other. He said that whenever he thought of me, his thoughts were the purest and most sincere. He said he was thinking about everything that could bring me comfort and pleasure, everything that could make me happier. He said that he would never spare any effort to give me everything. His greatest desire was to keep me in his heart, for the rest of his life.

Friday, November 18, 7:18 a.m.

I responded by saying I was happy to know they made it. I had looked at my phone all through the night, wondering if they were okay and if they had arrived safely.

End of Chapter Thoughts:

Dear Lord, You bring us out of the valleys and set our feet on mountain tops! Little did I know that this mountaintop was not one that God had designed for me. You see, we can be misled and deceived by the evil one and not even realize it. "Their flattery and fancy talk fool people who don't know any better" (Rom. 16:18 CEV). Yes, Satan disguises himself as "an angel of light" (2 Cor. 11:14 NLT), and I had fallen into his trap.

"Deeper and deeper, I sink into the mire; I can't find a foothold. I am in deep water and the floods overwhelm me" (Ps. 69:2 NLT).

I CONTINUED TO fall hard and fast. Do you remember the mudslide scene in "Romancing the Stone"? Michael Douglas and Kathleen Turner took a wild ride down the side of mountain and landed in a pool of cool, clear water. Well, I went right down a mudslide, but instead of a pool of cool, clear water, I landed in a deep, dark valley full of deceit, evil, and disgust.

After Jim arrived on the platform, the words of love, concern, affirmation, and tenderness continued. Jim shared pictures of the platform, the bunk room, the conference room, and himself in his bright orange work coveralls. There was something within me that flipped like a switch when Jim won the BP bid and headed off to work in the Gulf. My heart and my emotions had suddenly become entwined with him. But watch now for the beginning of a different twist to the plot.

Friday, November 18, 7:00 a.m.

I texted Jim and told him I realized he would be under a lot of pressure during his work on the platform and that I wouldn't text him anymore. I prayed for safety and told him I was full of joy and happiness. He responded by telling me how much he missed me and that it would be fine to continue to communicate with him. He said he had already taken his workers through the safety procedures and protocols. The food items would be delivered that day before five in the afternoon. He said that, as an independent contractor, he was in charge of taking care of his workers and making sure the contract was executed correctly. He said he would place a food order every five days and that it would be brought in by helicopter. He was responsible for making sure everyone had a healthy diet and strength to complete heavy work. Actually, he was laying the groundwork for a future issue. He told me he wouldn't be able to use the phone during work hours for security reasons and also because a phone's vibration could cause an explosion.

I told him to avoid causing an explosion and to just tell me about everything later!

Friday, November 18, 7:30 p.m.

Jim texted that he had barbecue ribs for dinner. The next day he would be preparing the drilling site. That would involve ensuring proper access and that the area had been properly graded for the placement of the rig and other equipment. After completing a survey, he would scuba dive in a steel cage to make sure the installation was done properly.

I responded: "Heavenly days! What exciting work! Be careful! Sounds dangerous to me! I'm praying for your safety and the safety of your team." Jim said that work would begin the next day and run from eight in the morning until seven in the evening, that he was sharing a room with one of his workers, that he would try to send pics the next day, and that equipment he had rented would be arriving on the platform shortly. I just took it all in and was fascinated by the whole operation.

Friday, November 18, 9:30 p.m.

The morning text from Jim said that when he thought of me, he felt loved, cared for, and calm. He said he missed being part of a couple and that he thought he had found his "happily ever after." He said he desired someone to tell secrets to and to lend a hand when he needed help. I admitted that I hadn't told any other person about him and that I was sorry that I was being so secretive. This was big Mistake No. 3 on my part! He reassured me that it was okay and that he knew I would feel more comfortable doing that after we met in person. I told him I missed having someone to share life with and to sometimes just do nothing, to sit on the porch and just be quiet, to take long walks with, to go to the kids' ballgames, to go get ice cream, to watch a movie, to cook and eat meals with, and to work together in the yard or garden. Jim responded by saying that these were beautiful moments he wanted to have with me. We talked about the beauty of the beach and the mountains and how much enjoyment comes from exploring there. I told him, "I love both, but the beach is the best. It's the roar of the ocean, the waves hitting my legs, the sand underneath my feet, and the warmth of the sun on my skin that touches my soul. And then there are the sunrises and sunsets that display God's creativity in a very special way."

Jim said that in every walk with nature, we receive far more than we seek. He asked if I liked flowers. I said, "Flowers make me happy! I even like wildflowers that grow along the road! I have a special memory of my son, Justin, gathering wildflowers along our road for Mother's Day. Best gift ever! I pick flowers that grow in my garden and put them in vases around the house to enjoy all the different colors.

I think I'm going to go crazy before I can see you! I don't want this feeling to ever go away!" Jim reassured me it would never go away and that he felt the same way too. He said he couldn't wait to bring me a bouquet of beautiful flowers.

Jim would be waking up early each morning for morning prayers with his workers. He would send me some prayers and Bible verses as well. He wanted to reassure me again, telling me how much he cared about me and expressing a genuine love for me. He knew these things were true by the butterflies in his stomach!

My comments were, "Sleep deep and wake up to a brand-new day! May God direct your way and give you wisdom and safety. I've got those butterflies too—I love it!!" Jim replied with wishes that I would sleep in the midst of angels. "Give thanks in all circumstances, for this is the will of God in Christ Jesus for you" (1 Thess. 5:16). Good night.

Saturday, November 19, 7:11 a.m.

I awoke to morning scriptures and prayers from Jim. I replied with, "Good morning! You are so precious and dear to me. Dear Lord, You are the bright and morning star! You created this earth and everything in it. I praise You this morning. Thank you for Jim and for sharing him with me. Please guide and protect his steps today. Protect the crew and keep unity among them. Help them accomplish their task even before the end of twenty days. May we be a reflection of Your Son. In Jesus' name, Amen."

The first of several photos from the platform began on this day.

One of the pictures of "Jim" on the platform. The other photos showed his face.

My reply: "Look at you! This is all so interesting to me. It surprises me that you have devotions with the guys. That's amazing! Do you lead the devotions?" Jim replied that he had put everything in the hands of God and that he would be leading devotions each morning before breakfast. I inquired about how the men received the devotions and if any of them believed Jesus is the Son of God and died for our sins. He said that most of them were believers.

Saturday, November 19, 7:34 p.m.

Jim let me know he was finished for the day and that he missed me. He asked if I had any fear. I thought that was a strange question, but I responded that I couldn't think of anything I was fearful of. He said that we shouldn't fear because God has not given us the spirit of fear but of power and love. I agreed and told him that "I prayed to find genuine love, to experience a love like I've never known. If this were to end tomorrow, it would have been worth it all." Jim replied that God answers prayers and that He had sent me as a jewel for him. He said he had found eternal love in me. I said, "I know He answers prayer but not necessarily the way we would plan. I had no intention of getting on Match. Only time will tell if you are the answer to my prayer."

I told him I had been wondering how a long-distance relationship would work when he finished his job and was living in Fayetteville. He replied that he was open to relocation and had nothing or anyone to keep him in Fayetteville. He said I was his everything, his queen, and he would be glad to buy a house close to me. I inquired about his contract work and what that would look like. He said he had a decision to make and that he was thinking about calling it quits after a long career. He said he was financially set and didn't need to work anymore. Jim expressed the desire to spend time with me and travel the world, helping the poor and telling others about Jesus. I replied, "I know your profile indicated you were planning for retirement in the near future. You know your financial situation. I don't want to influence you to do anything you're not ready for. You are healthy and probably have many years ahead of you. Let's pray together for God's wisdom in all of this." Jim agreed.

I asked, "How do you feel about my family? My grandchildren? It's a big family. As an only child, would you be comfortable? A big family is a lot of fun, and there are more people to love. My family means everything to me." Jim said he would be comfortable with everyone as long as they welcomed him with loving arms.

Sunday, November 20, 6:10 a.m.

The morning began as usual with the exchange of greetings and prayers. Then Jim said he was having difficulty getting into his bank account. He said he had tried over and over and couldn't access it, and it was possibly because of the poor internet connection out in the gulf. He asked if I would help him check his balance if he sent his online banking information. I was on my way to church and told him I would be happy to help him later. How could

I be so blind? He sent the song "Feels like a Blessing" by Benjamin Hastings and encouraged me to listen to it as I drove. He said he didn't have any doubts that he was a good man for me. I just drank in his lies!

Monday, November 21, 7:15 p.m.

Jim sent a long message about how having me by his side made him feel protected, capable of going down life's path, inflated with optimism and a hope that only a great love can bring. I was his dream come true. He was laying it on as thick as molasses, and again, I missed the clue. He was reeling me in like a fish on a hook by telling me one lie after another. Next, we moved on to getting into his bank account. He sent me the online banking information, his email, and his password "Godisgreat1" (Take a look at that password!). He asked me to insert the five-digit pin sent to my email address and check his account for any recent $170,000 deposit. It opened just like my banking online site.

Banking website looked like a regular online site

This is the information I saw when I opened the account:

Private Cargo Plane Transportation $350,000 11/15/22
Mobilization Fee services 4/30/22
ConocoPhillips Balance payment $2,250,800
Drilling Equipment Calaeinr Luminant Mining. Full
payment on extraction $1,823,400
Mark Lucas. Sales of parts. Oil Equipment Company,
Inc $754,610

Then there was a second page with more information; total balance $2,469,298.00 These numbers had no impact on me, even though it would have meant he was a millionaire!

I told Jim that he better hope I wasn't a crook! He laughed and said he trusted me and that I could trust him as well. He said trust is one of the key components of a successful relationship or marriage. He surely knew all the right things to say to tug at a girl's heartstrings!

I searched the same banking site as I was writing this book. SavingsCu.com is listed for sale! "Inquire now and SavingsCu.com can be yours today. This domain is listed for sale in the Unregister Market." Who knew you could buy your own online bank? Yes, he was a slick one!

Tuesday, November 22, 5:31 a.m.

My morning words to Jim, "Even before the morning of this new day breaks, I'm thinking of you and praying for you. Dear Lord, you are a miracle worker, the way maker, the bright and morning star! You bring us out of the valleys and set our feet on mountaintops! You hear us when we pray, and you give us good gifts. Jim is one of those good gifts! I thank you for him and his sweet, gentle spirit. I ask you to protect him and guide his steps. Open the door for success with his project and when it is complete, allow us to meet. Bless Jim today. I pray these things in Jesus' name, Amen." Jim thanked me for my prayer, and he responded with words of love and a prayer. He said to listen to Ed Sheeran's song "Perfect," that it was about me. Mistake Number 4: I did and it stirred my heart.

Tuesday, November 22, 2:30 p.m.

Jim sent an urgent message saying that there had been an accident on the platform caused by faulty equipment. He asked me to pray and said he would get back to me later. Little did I know that this was just him baiting the hook for what was to happen next.

Tuesday, November 22, 4:30 p.m.

Jim let me know that there had been no casualties but that the equipment would have to be replaced. His bank account had been placed on *posts only, no debits* due to suspicious login attempts. He said he would try to call his bank the next day.

Then he proceeded to talk about our first date, where to go, what I would like to do, and how each day would bring us closer to seeing each other. He said thoughts of me relieved his stress.

Wednesday, Nov 23, 7:37 a.m.

My morning prayer sent to Jim: "Good morning, friend! Dear Lord, I praise your high and holy name. You are the God of the universe, and by your hand you keep it in motion. Thank you for being a good, good God. Forgive me when I've failed or disappointed you. May we walk today as a reflection of your son. Take care of Jim today. May the work go smoothly without any problems or delay. Protect every single person on that platform. I ask that you help Jim with the banking issue and that it will be resolved quickly. Keep Jim under your wing of protection. In Jesus' name, Amen."

Jim replied with something like "Good morning, honey," and he thanked me for the prayer! He said he had just spoken with his bank, and it would take seven working days for his account to be rectified. He said his heart was broken because he needed to pay for the shipping fee and tax for equipment being shipped from Texas. Jim said he was supposed to pay $25,000 that day, and he could only come up with $10,000. I replied, "What's wrong with your banker?? The money is there! What can we do? I can wire you $15,000." Big Mistake No. 5! Where's my brain? Jim said that was nice of me and that he would send me the information so I could have a cashier check made out to an agent and put it in the mail. It should have been a red flag for me when he didn't even hesitate to take the money! He assured me I would get it back when he flew into Knoxville. I replied, "Okay, I'll head to town now. Do you need $15,000 even, or you want me to send the $25,000? Regular mail?" This was an even bigger mistake! I didn't even think twice about sending him money. After all, he needed help. Jim said to be sure and get a receipt with a tracking number. *I sent it*! Now, I'm not even going to share all the drama that occurred when I dropped it into a blue mailbox instead of sending it certified mail! I had to get a mailman to unlock the box and retrieve the envelope! Geez Louise!

Thursday, November 24, 5:32 a.m.

Jim's morning greeting was 1 Thessalonians 5:16–18 NIV, "Rejoice always, pray continually, give thanks in all circumstances; for this is God's will for you in Christ Jesus." He prayed to our dear loving Father that he was thankful for waking up this morning, for His love and care and for everything that He had freely given to him and his love, Janet. He also asked God to direct him to perform the work He had blessed his hands to do. He also thanked God for protecting him from anything that might come his way. He prayed protection over me as I went about my daily activities. He closed with Amen and God bless you, my love!

We exchanged greetings and chatted before he asked me what I thought my family would say about him. I replied that I thought they would be shocked. As it turned out, all of us were shocked at what I had done! Jim said he was happy that for once in his life he wouldn't be an only child because he would be part of my family. He said he could see the happiness and togetherness in my family and that he wanted to spend the rest of his life with me forever. I responded that it sounded amazing.

Then we started talking about pet peeves. He gave a short list which included drivers who don't use their turn signal; disrespect, especially of women; saying "I'm Fine" when they're actually not; and resorting to silent treatment when they are upset. I told him that he was insightful, and I agreed that people tend to wear a mask and pretend everything is okay when it's not. I told him I wanted him to always be upfront and truthful. I shared that it annoys me when people don't clean up after themselves and that I prefer people to volunteer to help rather than asking for help. Peeing on the floor and leaving hair in the shower are the worst!

Thursday, November 24, 11:17 p.m.

I felt such an excitement to think I had a second chance to find love. I texted the following: "I know you're sleeping—I'm not! Drinking hot chocolate and thinking nonstop about you. Looking at your pictures and seeing the change in your face from the post on Match to now, warms my heart. You have a sly little smile. I'm wondering if you will fly from Mexico to Knoxville when your job is completed. I can pick you up at the airport if you can fly here. Maybe you will be finished in time to stay a few days before I fly out on December 9. There are hotels close to the airport. If I hadn't already committed to this trip, I would just stay home. I want to spend time with you. I want to celebrate Christmas with you and to make plans for the days ahead. But I will understand if seeing you doesn't work out until later. I wouldn't like later, but I trust the Lord to orchestrate it all. It all feels so strangely wonderful! I hope this doesn't wake you up because I know how tired you are and how much you need your sleep."

Thursday, November 24, 6:01 a.m.

Jim responded that he had thought about flying into Knoxville when he left Mexico and that he wanted to do that. He said he hadn't mentioned it because he didn't know how I would feel about that. He said he was happy I was feeling that way too. Jim said he believed our meeting was divine and that I was sent from heaven. He said he woke up feeling so happy and blessed!

Here comes the next bait! He knew my heart was soft! Jim texted that they were about to run short on food. He said he was supposed to make an order, but he couldn't do that due to his bank account being locked. Then he quickly changed the subject back to me picking him up at the airport and wondered if I would be free. I asked him which day, and he replied that it would be between the sixth or seventh. Put a pin in those dates.

Then I asked, "What will you do for food? You have to eat to keep your strength up." Then I made the next big mistake—Mistake No. 7. He proceeded to tell me I was the sweetest being he had ever met in his life! Then he dropped the bomb! Jim wanted to know if it was possible for me to get cash and mail it to an agent responsible for the food delivery. He said it needed to be cash because he was in a rush to order the food, and a cashier check would take a couple of days before the cash would be available. I didn't know if that's true or not, but I believed him. He proceeded to tell me it would be okay if I couldn't help him. When I asked him how much he needed, a red flag should have gone up at $15,000. I told him I had $18,000 in my account and that I could send it after the bank opened at 9:00 a.m. I replied that $15,000 sure was a large amount for food. He reminded me that it had to be flown in by helicopter and that drove up the price.

Jim proceeded to tell me that he loved me and that I was the light in his life. He said God's love would never leave my life and was looking forward to experiencing the beauty of life with me. Then, I ran to the bank and mailed *cash* in a certified mailer! I had completed Mistake No. 8. My brain had left me!

Friday, November 25, 12:01 p.m.

I sent this text: "Okay, you have my money and my heart; what else is left?" Jim reassured me my heart and money were safe with him and that I would be getting back every penny. I responded that I was going to be in big trouble if we finally met and didn't like each other. He said that wasn't possible because his heart was with me one hundred percent. I just kept believing the lies. I told him that if the table were turned and it was one of my children in my position, I would be telling them to take their time and not get in a rush. I am normally a rational person! I have displayed a lot of common sense in the past, and I have three degrees from the University of Tennessee, for what that's worth!

Saturday, November 26, 7:37 a.m.

Jim started the day with a prayer, asking the Lord to bless me, to give me good health, love, and a lifetime of happiness. He prayed that our faith would grow in Him and that we would have the courage to pursue our dreams.

As we continued to pray together and to learn more about each other, I fell deeper into the pit!

Sunday, November 27, 1:59 p.m.

I texted Jim after hearing the sermon at church, which was based on Psalm 23. The part about Him restoring our soul—I told Jim I thought God was restoring my soul through him. Some of the brokenness caused by David's death was being replaced with a little joy.

Sunday, November 27, 3:51 p.m.

Jim replied that Psalm 23 was one of his favorite chapters in the Bible. He wanted to know if I would ever take him to church with me. I responded: "Why not? I would love that! I don't need or want expensive things or to go on extravagant trips. I just want someone who loves the Lord and loves me second." We continued to chat, and then round three disaster began.

Sunday, November 27, 7:51 p.m.

Jim texted that God is great and had protected the crew when there was an explosion on the platform caused by faulty equipment. Red flags again. The same scenario as before. Jim said he didn't want to bug me with his problems. I replied, "Please do! Then I will know what to pray for!

Dear Lord, we need this equipment to be repaired quickly so the work can be completed on time. This is our request, but we trust You and Your timing! In Jesus' name, Amen."

Monday, November 28, 5:09 p.m.

Jim texted that the work had stalled! The engineers had not been able to repair the equipment, and they couldn't risk causing another explosion. He said it was a disappointing day and that it would probably delay his arrival in Knoxville. Jim reminded me that his deadline was December 8 and that he would only be allowed a one-week extension. He was pulling at my heartstrings because he knew how much I was looking forward to meeting him at the airport. I said, "That's the second time the equipment has caused a problem. What do you do now about the equipment that's broken?" Why did I think I needed to fix the problem? Because I'm wired that way!

Then he began to explain that it was the mud pump equipment which he just couldn't do without. He could get it cheaper if he bought it from China but that would take seven days, and that was out of the equation. He indicated that he could get it in the States and resell it after the project. All the rental equipment was always worn out. He had a busting headache and thanked me for listening and being his best friend.

Tuesday, November 29, 10:00 a.m.

Jim texted to say he had called his bank and that he was very irritated by their response. They told him his case had been forwarded to fraud prevention and security department. For his own safety, they required him to appear in person at the bank to resolve the issue. Here was Warning Sign No. 7, and I missed it. I texted back: "Can they not just verify who you are? Is it because you're out of the country? Is it a new account?" Jim replied that he had opened his account there over a year ago. He didn't know which way to turn, but he knew everything happens for a reason. It would cost him close to $75,000, including shipping, to purchase the new equipment. I replied, "Holy Moly! I have one more savings account that has $75,319." My heart of compassion overruled my thinking, again!

Jim asked if I was willing to send the $75,000. He said that if I was willing to help him then just send $35,000 the next day, and once it was ready to ship, then he would have me send the balance. Warning Sign No. 8 should have been that he had no hesitation to take the money or any concern about my resources. I told him I would send it. There was total and complete lack of judgment on my part. I had no concern about loaning him the money, which was a total and incomplete lack of any judgment. I had no concern about giving it all to him. He said I shouldn't feel sorry for him but that I should just pray for him.

So I did: "Dear Lord Jesus, I praise you for the good Father that you are. I lift up Jim to you and ask you to guide, direct, and intervene in this project so that these obstacles may be overcome and the work completed on time. Comfort Jim and give him peace and calm that he may trust you for all things. You are all powerful and all things are possible through you. I pray these things in Jesus' name, Amen."

He said, Amen and amen and that reading my prayer had brought calmness to his soul and that he felt very confident about everything. Looking back, I would say, Yeah, I bet you were!

"The light (Jesus) shines in the darkness, and darkness has not overcome it" (John 1:5 NIV).

GOD PREVENTED ME from falling any deeper into this valley. He turned on the light, and the darkness could not overcome it. God's intervention is when He causes something to happen or when He prevents something from happening. On the day I was to send the $75,000, the money was transferred from one bank to another, and I hadn't realized it wouldn't be available for three days. Also, He physically sent one of His children to turn on the light!

Wednesday, November 30, 6:03 a.m.

My morning text sent to Jim: "Dear Lord, I praise you this morning. You are the maker of heaven and earth and everything in it. You created Jim, and you created me. We seek your wisdom and guidance in these days that lay ahead of us. May we live our lives in a way that is pleasing to you. Thank you for Jim, my best friend.

Surround us with love and happiness for the rest of our earthly days. Protect him today and give him strength. In Jesus' name, Amen."

Jim, I transferred the money to my bank, but it won't be available until Friday! I'm trying to scrape up some from checking. Just need to look at when auto payments happen. Can you still come up with $10,000? I can only do $20,000." Jim replied to just send $25,000 cash via the same mailing process as before.

Wednesday, November 30, 8:00 a.m.

(My daughter-in-law (DNL) called and said, "I need to talk to you; I'll be right up." She sat down on the couch and apologized for accidentally seeing my text message come up on her phone as she was checking our phone bill. We have shared a phone plan for twelve years, and this had never happened before. With nervous tension in her eyes she asked, "Who are you sending $25,000 to?" I felt violated, but I proceeded to tell her I had fallen in love with a man I had never met and that he needed help. She questioned every detail about the situation and then looked me in the eye and said, "I'm sorry, but this is a scam! Don't send him the money. I beg you to not send the money!" She continued passionately to try to talk some sense into me. I listened, but I couldn't convince myself to believe it. After she left, I went straight to the bank and sent $25,000 *cash*! Blinded by love! Oh, dear me! The Lord intervened in my blindness through my loving, caring, smart daughter-in-law, Whitney, but I was so intertwined with this charade that I couldn't think rationally.

Thursday, December 1, 4:58 a.m.

I sent Jim a text: "Sleepless in Tennessee! I need to talk to you when you can." Right away Jim asked if I was okay, and I responded that I was confused. I told him about the conversation that I had with Whitney and how embarrassed I felt. I told him I was struggling. He told me he just wanted me to be calm and pray. He asked if I had sent the money, and I told him I had sent $25,000 cash. I said, "If you're a scammer, then you are a darn good one!" Jim asked me not to talk that way and said Whitney had invaded our privacy. I told him she would never have done that on purpose and that it was an accident. Jim asked me to trust him as always and to not have any negative thoughts about him.

Thursday, December 1, 3:52 p.m.

Jim checked in with me to see how I was doing. He said he had just tracked the money, and it was still in the USPS possession at the Maryville location. It was not in transit yet.

Thursday, December 1, 4:00 p.m.

DNL: Okay, just see what happens with this man when you don't send him the money. See how he responds and reacts and just take it out of the equation. I am willing to bet the farm that this is fake, and I'm so sorry to say that. So many parts of this story don't add up, and BP is a worldwide company. He is most likely a professional scam artist and probably makes good money doing this. I hope I'm wrong for your sake, but please don't send any money to him and see what happens to the relationship.

Janet: I hope you're wrong too! (I just couldn't tell her I had already sent the money.)

DNL: People are scammed on those sites especially, and they have answers for everything. He contacted you first, right, and pretty quick? They are professionals. Protect yourself at all costs, sort of like walk softly but carry a big stick.

Thursday, December 1, 9:00 p.m.

DNL: I have a very bad feeling about this that I can't shake. The picture that you sent to me is fraudulent. That is photoshopped. Please be careful with this person. I pray you didn't send them money.

Janet: Why do you say photoshopped? What do you see?

DNL: The name and the piece of paper are both photoshopped. The BP is not correct logo or centered and the person's name is wavy and not lined up correctly. This is a picture of a meeting but could be any meeting, and those papers could be any papers at all and were tampered with through editing.

Janet: I don't know how to Photoshop, so I can't see it like you do.

DNL: Look closely. Not centered or professional and waviness on name, and they never ever would send someone on a job two days later. If you win a bid, it could take as long as months or as quick as thirty to forty days.

So many things don't add up. If you sent something to them, stop it at the next destination. If he's questioned you about the money multiple times or become upset at all, that's a red flag. I know you think I'm crazy, but I promise I'm just trying to protect you. Also, the water bottle labels are blurred out. Completely fake picture.

Janet: I don't think you're crazy, and I appreciate you helping work through these things. It's good to get fresh eyes on it.

DNL: Janet, I am not saying this lightly. I feel this is a one thousand present scam, and you need to be very, very careful. Did you send this person money?

Janet: Yes.

DNL: Go to the bank tomorrow or the mail and find out how to stop it. Go to the police, and tell them you've been scammed! I don't want to see you hurt anymore, and this person will drop you so fast as soon as they get the money.

Janet: I'm praying for guidance on this.

DNL: Please trust me on this, I beg you. You know me. You don't know them. I would not be saying this if I didn't feel the way I do about it. I would bet that if you asked anyone else, they would tell you the same.

Janet: I know they would.

DNL: I know this must hurt and be hard for you, but there's absolutely no reason not to believe me. Do whatever you need to do to stop that from getting there. There was a reason I was supposed to see those messages. It was to protect you from this or worse.

Janet: I've already told myself that same thing.

DNL: Really stop and think about that. The exact timing of that! Fill out the Intercept form at the PO.

Janet: I just now did that online. It should return to the Kellar Lane Post Office in Maryville.

DNL: I'm so proud of you. Everything will be okay. We will just have to do some work on your heart to heal from this devil.

Thursday, December 1, 9:10 p.m.

Jim texted again to check on me. I told him I was sick to my stomach and couldn't talk. He was very upset and prayed for me. He said he was afraid I was sick because of what had happened with Whitney. I didn't respond. He continued to text his concerns, scriptures, and prayers. What happens when an evil person prays?

Okay, I finally got it! I acknowledged that he was a scammer. I decided that I would play along but do everything in my power to witness to this evil man. I thought about this passage: "As the rain and the snow come down from heaven, and do not return to it without watering the earth and making it bud and flourish, so that it yields seed for the Sower and bread for the eater, so is my word that goes out from my mouth: It will not return to me empty, but will accomplish what I desire and achieve the purpose for which I sent it" (Isa. 55:10–11 NIV). I vowed to myself that I would not send him any more money, and I wouldn't mourn over what I had already sent. The money he had taken from me would be worth it if a soul were saved!

Friday, December 2, 2:49 a.m.

My morning text to Jim: "I'm thinking about you and wondering if you've been able to sleep. You work so hard at what you do. I'm not throwing up anymore, but my body is weak. My mind is strong, and I'll be okay. I'm so glad you know Jesus, and we can look forward to a life without pain and suffering. This world is so full of evil people that sadly will spend eternity burning in hell. We can't even comprehend what eternity is or how horrible hell will be. You've never told me your wife's name, but you would see her again if she accepted Jesus as her Lord. Was she a born-again Christian? Have you been baptized? Christening as a baby doesn't count. Will the food shipment be delivered today?"

Friday, December 2, 7:04 a.m.

Jim began to answer my questions. He said his wife's name was Ella and she was a born-again Christian. He said he had been baptized because "He who has believed and has been baptized shall be saved, but he who has disbelieved shall be condemned" according to Mark 16:16.

He said the shipment would arrive before the end of the day by God's grace. Then he wanted to talk about what had happened yesterday concerning the confrontation with Whitney. I told him I had an eye appointment I needed to get to and that I was feeling much better. By the way, I bought Christmas presents for you yesterday."

The sad part was, I really did. I was just living the fantasy! I ended our conversation with a prayer: "Dear Lord, You are the way, the truth, and the life. Thank you for loving us so much that You gave Your only Son so that we may live a life beyond the grave. Forgive our sins as we are all sinners and mess up every day. Walk close to Jim. Guide him, protect him physically *and* from the evil of this world. Thank you for his life and use him as Your witness as he leads his crew. In Jesus' name, Amen."

Friday, December 2, 11:50 a.m.

Janet to DNL: I went to the sheriff's office, but they weren't all that interested. Said there is nothing they can do. Didn't even ask my name or address.

DNL: I called and talked to them too. They told me nothing they could do if he didn't steal it. It's not theft if you willingly give it. Do you have a picture of this guy? I am going to see if he has a record and see if we have any chance of catching him so he doesn't do this again. I can run his photo across a database and it shows if he has other profiles. (Photo sent) I am showing he has three profiles with the phone number listed. Yep. That's him. I found him. He's operating from the Dallas Airport and lives in San Antonio, Texas. This, of course, is not his real name or phone number. He uses all different ones.

Janet: SICKENING!

DNL: He is associated with a Hispanic lady who is seventy, named A.M. and many other names. This just goes on and on. I'm exhausted.

Janet: You missed your calling, Whitney; you're a detective!

DNL: I prefer private investigator! LOL It's not the same person you are talking to. It's fake. Have him video chat you again or FaceTime and let it be clear as a bell. Don't hike into something that isn't real.

Janet: I won't. I've learned my lesson. I must be the naivest person ever! (Jim sent a copy of his passport by text. I forwarded it to Whitney.) He's trying to prove his identity through this passport! Anything can be fabricated.

DNL: That's totally *fake*! I bet he's wondering where that money is today! I bet he's upset as all get out.

Janet: Makes me physically ill.

DNL: I'm sorry! This is why I don't like people. I am called to love everyone as Jesus does, but I don't trust anyone because of stuff like this.

Janet: I'm just the opposite! I trust everyone. Obviously not always a good thing. I'm just too naive!

Friday, December 2, 9:56 p.m.

DNL: I'm so sorry. I'm sorry about everything. I'm sorry you're obviously upset with me. I am here for you. If they're in the US, you could press charges. We have a name and address where the money went. Something to think about. I don't know if you would want to ever meet these crooks though.

Janet: I am not upset with you! I am so very thankful that you care enough about me to not give up.

My DNL sent me a copy of a news article about a woman in Canada who was scammed out of $300,000 by an oil rigger (https://globalnews.ca/news/2357608/senior-swindled-out-of-300000-in-online-romance-scam/).

When I read the article, it was as if I was reading a story about myself! It was almost as if Jim had followed a script. I was finally convinced that my daughter-in-law was right, and the truth was so very evident. Thank you, Lord, for intervening through Whitney and for her dogged persistence to rescue me!

Saturday, December 3, 1:00 p.m.

Jordan, my third son, showed up unexpectedly at my house without his children to blow leaves off the porch. When I told him I needed to talk to him, the flood gates opened, and I sobbed as I confessed what I had done. He was so tender and sweet and kept telling me it didn't matter what I had done, that everything would be okay. He said "We are all here for you and love you. We'll get through it." Then he called his new FBI friend for advice.

I continued to keep Jim on the hook as I tried to figure out my options. I knew right away that I didn't want my DNL to track him down. I didn't want to press charges if he was found. I fully realized that I wouldn't recover any of the $40,000, but I was praying that the other $25,000 would actually be intercepted and returned to me.

Saturday, December 3, 3:00 p.m.

DNL: I am praying for peace that surpasses all understanding for all of us. Ready to be done with this mess!

Janet: Waiting for a call back from USPS customer service.

Around 3:30 p.m., I received a call from USPS which verified the certified mail had been intercepted and would be shipped back to Maryville. Praise the Lord! That evening I met with my other two sons and their wives and shared my mistakes. They were supportive and loving, and it felt great to have them share this huge burden. The next day, I FaceTimed with my daughter and son-in-law in Kentucky. Now all my immediate family knew how I had succumbed to the scam and fallen into this pit. They saw me at my worst. What a humbling, embarrassing experience this was for me. It was if there had been a role reversal, and I was the kid!

I knew in my intellectual brain that Jim was a fraud, but my emotions were still so tied to him that I couldn't let him go. I did begin to challenge his statements and his intentions to see if he would squirm. Two of my sons had recently met an FBI agent who attended their church. They separately reached out to him, and he encouraged me to file FBI and USPS fraud reports. I did.

Saturday, December 3, 9:00 p.m.

I texted Jim, "See if you can figure another way to get the rest of the money for the equipment." Jim said he already had and was not successful. He wondered why I was changing my mind and asked if I was thinking I wouldn't get my money back. He reassured me he had kept calculations and that I would get every penny back. I responded, "I realized I need money for a payment due the first part of the month and with Christmas expenses and my Florida trip, I need to be able to cover my own obligations. I want to help you more, but I know you will understand." Jim kept trying to convince me that he would repay me as soon as he got to the States and that he only needed $50,000 more to finish the project. He said he realized I was struggling because of what my daughter-in-law was telling me and that he understood, but she was wrong. I told him it would absolutely break my heart if he ever mistreated me.

Jim said that when I send the money, to send cash. He would finish the project and be in Knoxville by December 8. I replied, "I told you on the phone I can't send it." I had made the decision that he would get no more money from me, and I put it in stone! He texted back that God would take control and sent the following scripture: "Take up the shield of faith, with which you can extinguish all the flaming arrows of the evil one" from Ephesians 6:16 NIV."

I'm not sure who he was referring to as the "evil one," but I held on to this verse and reminded myself that the enemy is always seeking to attack us through doubt, temptation, and deception to cause us to fall. Yes, God is faithful to provide and protect.

Saturday, December 3, 9:45 p.m.

Jim texted that he was crushed but trying to stay calm. He didn't know how he would get the $50,000, and he couldn't understand why I was having a change of heart toward him. He said he realized it wasn't my responsibility. He said he missed me, and he missed my laugh.

I texted Jim back and told him I had talked to a friend from Match.com and learned that he was still active on the site. He denied it and said she didn't know what she was talking about. Jim said there are people who just want to destroy other's happiness. He wondered why all of this was happening to him and questioned why I would really believe her over his word? He asked me just to trust him. I replied, "Trust is built over time. When everything falls into place like you say, then I'll know without a doubt I can trust you. I've known her for a long time, and she has no reason to make this up. I could reactivate and search for your profile, but I'm not going to do that." My friend on Match.com was really my daughter-in-law, my own private investigator!

Sunday, December 4, 4:04 a.m.

"The Lord is my rock, my fortress, and my savior; my God is my rock, in whom I find protection. He is my shield, the power that saves me, and my place of safety. He is my refuge, my savior, the one who saves me from violence" (2 Sam. 22:2–3 NLT).

The practical, intelligent side of me knew better but the emotional, loving, caring side of me wanted so badly to believe Jim was not a fraud. The rawness of the death of my husband, my companion, my lover, allowed me to live in this fantasy world. In this fantasy world, I was not lonely.

"Jim, I gave you my heart and my money. I loved who I thought you were. How can you rob widows of their life savings and then sleep at night? How can you live with yourself? You are not who you say you are!" His response questioned the meaning of those statements, and he wondered why on earth I would say those things to him! He said that we had connected by video call, I had seen his driver's license, and he was really amazed by what I had said. He assured me he hadn't robbed me of anything and that I would get every penny back. I responded, "The video call was of no value, a few minutes and poor quality. People make fake driver's licenses every day! Your picture is on another man's Facebook page. He's a realtor in Philadelphia, Pennsylvania." He explained this by saying that someone had stolen his identity. He was astonished that I would believe this lie and add this extra burden on him with all he was going through on the platform. I responded, "I so badly want to believe you, but at this point you will have to prove it." Dear Lord, I lift up this situation to you! I ask you to reveal the truth. You know all and see all, and I trust you. Turn this confusion to clear sight and shine your light on the evil. In Jesus' name, Amen. "If I'm wrong, Jim, I will apologize with all my being, but as for now, you will have to prove yourself."

Sunday, December 4, 8:12 a.m.

Jim was angry. He said the devil is a liar and was trying to come between us. He sent more Bible verses and prayers. He said he was a failure, but that he wanted me to be strong and not give up on us because my efforts would be rewarded. He asked what kind of proof I needed and I said, "Kind of like what you said your bank told you—to see you in person!" I believed God was working in his heart through all of this. I might never see the results, but I prayed for his lost soul. We should never underestimate the power God has to take a life in a new direction.

Monday, December 5, 10:00 a.m.

Jim had been tracking the money and realized the package had been intercepted by the post office. He immediately asked me why I stopped it. I replied, "Why do you think I stopped it? Just watch the other man's videos on Facebook. Then explain that to me!" He lost his patience with me and said he wouldn't beg me or try to prove his innocence anymore. He said for me to do whatever pleased me and that I had done something beyond explanation. He had never expected such from me. This was the first time he had ever lost his patience with me. I guess I had lost a little patience myself when I responded, "That's your face on Facebook, but it's not your voice on the video. I was so stupid to fall into your trap. Yes, you're right. I had a change of heart when I saw these things. I didn't want to believe it, but I now know the truth." Jim wished me well and said he had my address and would be sending all the money back to me. I replied, "If that happens, then I will praise the Lord, and my trust will be restored." Jim said, "Go ahead and praise your Lord." Then he flipped a switch and began to tell me how much he cared about me but that I had broken his heart. I told him, "I have given to you more than I have ever given to anyone! I am worthless right now. I can't think straight, do anything; I can hardly function." That was, in fact, the truth. I was an emotional wreck.

Jim asked me again to allow the money to go through. He said he would swear on his wife's grave that he would repay me. Then he would give thanks to God.

Tuesday, December 6, 6:12 a.m.

Jim started the day by asking if I would ever forget him. I replied, "You stole my money, my heart, my freedom, and my peace of mind! No, I'll never forget you. When my roof needs to be replaced, I'll think of you. When my car stops running and needs to be replaced, I'll think of you! When disaster hits and I need $40,000, I'll think of you! My youngest and oldest sons live on either side of me, but that's not enough now. My twenty-year-old grandson is moving in with me and bringing his shotgun! An elaborate security system is being installed. The police have been contacted. In one month, my life has been destroyed!"

Jim demanded that I calm down and stop saying all these things. He questioned if I really believed that he would come and hurt me. I replied, "Did you read the Global news article? It's almost step by step what you did, like you followed a play book. You know how close my family is. They are very concerned. I'm grieving the loss of my husband and now the loss of 'Jim.' All I do now is cry."

Jim said he was angry that my family was more important to me than he was. I replied, "You have followed evil. You have hurt me and stolen from me, but I will not retaliate. The apostle Paul says, "Do not repay anyone evil for evil. Be careful to do what is right in the eyes of everyone." Also, "Do not take revenge, my dear friends, but leave room for God's wrath, for it is written: 'It is mine to avenge; I will repay,' says the Lord" (Rom. 12:17,19 NIV). Jim, it is not too late to repent and turn from your evil ways. You can be forgiven. Your eternal life is more important than money!" There was no response from Jim.

My end-of-the-day thoughts: Jim was a liar, a deceiver, and a thief! God is the Father of truth; Satan is the father of lies. No wonder God hates deceit and deceivers. When our words are deceptive and deceitful, we reflect a heart that is submitted to Satan. Deceptive words reveal a heart that is not for God but against God. Jesus said, "But the words you speak come from the heart—that's what defiles you. For from the heart come evil thoughts, murder, adultery, all sexual immorality, theft, lying, and slander. These are what defile you" (Matt. 15:18–20 NLT). Is there any hope for deceivers? Most certainly! In Ephesians 4:22, Paul tells us it is possible to get rid of the old way of life and live a new life. Deceivers can become righteous by the grace of Jesus. Even the most deceptive deceiver can be forgiven and changed. Yes, even Jim!

"I lift up my eyes to the mountains, where does my help come from? My help comes from the LORD, the Maker of heaven and earth. He will not let your foot slip, he who watches over you will not slumber; indeed, he who watches over Israel will neither slumber nor sleep. The LORD watches over you, the LORD is your shade at your right hand; the sun will not harm you by day, nor the moon by night. The LORD will keep you from all harm, he will watch over your life; the LORD will watch over your coming and going both now and forevermore." (Ps. 121:1–8, NIV)

I CONTINUED TO slowly find footholds as I ascended out of the valley toward the summit.

Jim and I both continued to track the parcel but for very different reasons. He was going to push me to resend it to him, and I was just praying I'd be able to put it back in my bank account. He continued to tell me how much he loved me and wanted to spend the rest of his life with me. We continued to pray together and read scriptures together. Finally, a week after I had originally sent the parcel, I received an email saying it was back in Maryville and ready for pick up. I rushed to the post office, wondering if any of the cash would be in the package. After the clerk handed me the package (actually the same clerk that had several months back handed me my husband in a box!), I ran to the car and took out the contents of the package. Yes, there was cash! I spread it out over my lap and counted all $25,000. It was quite a pile of 100-dollar bills. Thank you, my Lord. You had rescued me from further shame and destruction. As soon as Jim could tell from the tracking that I had received the parcel, he was on me to return it to him.

$25,000 in 100-dollar bills

Tuesday, December 6, 5:45 a.m.

My text to Jim: "Good morning! Dear Lord, as we start this new week, I hold on to the promise that You said You would never leave or forsake us. You said You would lead us beside still waters and restore our souls. Thank you for restoring my soul and putting the broken pieces back together. As Jim said in his prayer, may I spread the fruit of the Holy Spirit wherever You lead me today. Wherever Jim goes today, direct his path, protect him from harm, draw his spirit to You. Please forgive us for the times we take our eyes off of you and do wrong. Give us joy and peace. In Jesus' name, Amen. Have a day filled with joy!"

Jim replied, Amen and amen! Then he proceeded to say that there had been a breakage in one of the pipes connected to the storage tank. He was thankful that there was no spillage, but work would be halted until equipment could be obtained. Yet, another problem! I told him to try to get it on credit, and he said that wasn't possible. He told me to pack my bags and go to Florida and have fun; he would keep me posted on everything. He said he loved me and wanted to share the same faith, same belief, and trust.

I replied, "I'm going to Florida to serve as a chaplain. I'll be there to pray with people who have been impacted by Hurricane Ian. It will be fun, but it's not a vacation; I won't be walking on the beach. Thank you for keeping me posted on your progress. You can accomplish your work!"

Jim became defensive and said he would let me decide our fate and that he felt his best was not good enough. He proceeded to say he didn't like how he was being treated, and he couldn't understand why I didn't trust him. Jim said he would never keep my money and that not only did it help him but it helped others.

I prayed: "Dear Lord, I lift your name on high; You are the one who sees all and knows all. Your Word tells us that we must all come before You to be judged. Second Corinthians 4:10 says we will each receive whatever we deserve for the good or the evil we have done. Please forgive me for trying to do life on my own and without totally depending on you. I come before You today, asking you to give Jim and I clarity in this situation to guide both of us to know the truth, for the truth will set us free. Keep Jim close to you and keep him safe. Work in his spirit and fill him with joy. Help him to know I desire nothing but the best for him. In Jesus' name, Amen."

Then Jim said he needed to get off the platform as soon as possible. He said he was willing to leave everything and come to me before I left for Florida. It would cost him $15,000 to take a helicopter from the platform to Merida, purchase an airline ticket to Maryville, and get a hotel. He asked if I could send him travel money.

I replied, "That's too expensive for one day. We've waited this long, so a couple more weeks won't make that much difference."

As he continued to pressure me for more money, I began to feel a little concerned. Thoughts of someone showing up at my home to physically harm me or my family began to haunt me. I needed to form some type of boundary for protection. During his next phone call, I told him that my kids thought I had lost my ability to make wise decisions, that I'd lost my mind! Now I have to turn control of my finances over to them, and I will only have access to $3,000 a month. That was not true, but I did feel like my life had spiraled out of control and I was a helpless mess! I asked the Lord to please forgive me for succumbing to fear and lies. It was only through God's strength that I could resist the lies of the evil one. By the way, Jim was furious!

Wednesday, December 7, 6:45 p.m.

Jim wanted to know if I had deposited the $25,000 that was returned to me. He said for me to send it to him so he could come home to me. He said he was giving up his contract, that he was a loser and a failure. I replied, "Yes, it's back in the bank. Do you not remember my son is temporarily in charge of my bank account? I can't send you any more money. I have no way to help you. I wish this were all so different; that you didn't get the contract, that you didn't go to the platform, and that I could have met you face-to-face a month ago. Your bank should have been able to verify your identity through security questions and cell number. That doesn't make sense that they told you to come in person." He couldn't believe I wasn't going to help him. Then he said he just wanted me to be happy. He said I should find a man that my children would love and that he wasn't that man. He said he was walking away from everything we had ever had. Jim said there was no need to fight for something that was already gone. He told me that my children had made the decision for me, and that in their eyes, he was a nobody, a bad egg. Jim said his health was suffering because of the whole issue and that he wouldn't be communicating with me anymore. He said I would be receiving a check for $40,000 so he could clear his conscience. I replied, "I'm not gone. I don't want to let you go! You know who I am, where I am, and everything about me, my dreams and hopes. You are the one letting go. Take care of yourself. I guess this must be goodbye. I'll miss you so much." I knew now that I wasn't really "in love" with this imposter but the truth was, I would miss him. He had been a distraction from my loneliness. He had filled a void. He had taken my hope of finding a Christian man and falsely filled each and every dream.

Thursday, December 8, 7:08 a.m.

Jim was supposed to have arrived at the Knoxville airport on this day. Of course, that had always been a lie. Jim texted to let me know he had overcome the pain, torture, and agony he had passed through because of me. He said that he hadn't been treated fairly but that he was well and mentally strong again. It's amazing to me how that happened just overnight! He said he still cared about me, but he wouldn't be texting or calling anymore. I replied, "Well, I'm not healed. I'm having to relive the memories of my husband's COVID and death during this time last year. Now I'm having to grieve the loss of you at the same time. Please don't treat my heart like a yo-yo. It's hard for me to believe you think I've mistreated you!" Then Jim proceeded to say he couldn't live without me, that I was already in his heart forever.

Friday, December 9, 10:08 a.m.

I was waiting at the airport to fly to Florida to do volunteer work when the postal inspector called. He was very gentle with me and he requested copies of all the certified mail receipts. I had copies on my phone that I forwarded to him. He said he would review them, and we would talk again after I returned. That meant I needed to hold on to my conversation with Jim for ten more days.

December 10–December 15

So, the daily conversations continued morning and night. He continued to tell me how much I meant to him and how he couldn't live without me. Then he dropped another bomb!

Friday, December 16, 6:15 a.m.

Jim texted that he would be needing me in order for him to return to the states. He would be getting his paycheck, but it would be a large sum of money and would take ten days to clear his bank. He promised to repay me everything as soon as he landed in Knoxville. I replied, "You know my hands are tied! Dear Lord, thank you for a glorious new day! Your mercies are new each morning. Your word says that repentance is admitting wrongdoing and saying you're sorry. It involves us understanding how our actions have caused pain and suffering to another person. Forgiveness is pardoning someone who has hurt us. We are all sinners and hurt others without even knowing it. Please forgive me this morning for wrong thoughts or words. Protect Jim and his crew today. Guard his heart and his actions as he brings this project to a close. In Jesus' name, Amen. Have an awesome day!" Jim texted back that I meant the world to him and that I was the best thing that had ever happened to him. He promised that helping the man you love was not a bad thing and that he would never let me down.

I told him, "This has been a tough ride but I'm holding on to Jesus. Could you contact your bank for a loan or put a lien on your car?" Of course, his answer was negative because all he wanted was for me to send him more money. I became a broken record telling him each time he asked that I couldn't loan him any more money. The amount he asked for began to dwindle each time he had a need. The latest amount was $10,000. I told him to "Trust in the Lord. I don't know how but if it is His will, He will make a way. The Bible tells us that His thoughts are higher than our thoughts, and His ways are higher than ours. He is all knowing and all powerful, and He is sovereign over all."

Jim began to tell me in every possible way how I was his one and only true love, his angel, his life, his entire world, his sweet wine. He said he loved me so deeply and knew that was true because there was no one else his heart beat for. And on and on it went. I knew none of it was true and that he was only trying to soften my heart.

Saturday, December 17, 8:02 a.m.

My question for Jim: "Does your heart ever break to think about what will happen to all those who have never accepted Jesus as Lord? To think the liars, thieves, adulterers, sexually immoral will go to hell and suffer tortured lives burning in hell for eternity (Based on 1 Corinthians 6:9)?" Jim didn't answer my question but confirmed that in spite of all God has done to save people, they follow Satan right into the fiery abyss. Jim was never so right!

Then Jim proceeded to tell me I was unique and special and then he asked me to marry him!

I replied, "Oh my! You should check me out first! I'm sure you know about buying used cars! Would you buy one sight unseen?"

Jim said I was so funny but that I had a heart of gold. He said that I came into his life like a star and filled his heart with joy. I took his pain as if it were mine and gave him a shoulder to cry on. I had become his pillar of strength whenever he felt low and made his life on earth worth living. He said that I had made his life on earth worthwhile. I gave light to his soul, and I was his angel from above. On and on his discourse went as he tried to reel in my heart as if it were a prize-winning fish!

Sunday, December 18, 2:13 p.m.

Jim texted that there were a lot of things he was concerned about, and one of them was the food supply wouldn't last much longer. He was at it with the food scenario again! He knew my weakness! I asked the Lord to help me be strong! He said he felt like he was a burden to me. I replied, "I don't feel like you are a burden. You make me happy until you ask for money that I don't have to give. You know I'm a giving person and generous with what I have. It makes me sad that I can't help you anymore." He questioned why I didn't want to help the man I loved when he was in dire need; did his happiness not matter to me? Did I think he would turn his back on me if the tables were turned?

I responded: "Yes, your happiness matters to me! Why are you trying to put a guilt trip on me?? I've explained over and over about my financial situation. You surely understand, and you know I've always been truthful with you. How can I give you something I don't have?" That was true. I didn't have any more money that I should just give to a scammer.

As he continued to try and make me feel guilty, he said, I could make a sacrifice for the person I loved. I asked him, "What do you suggest I sacrifice? My house? My car?" He remembered the transfer of $75,000 from my savings and the $25,000 that was intercepted. He promised to pay back every dime. Like a broken record, I repeated, "Again, my kids have temporarily tied my hands from getting any money. They think my head is fogged because of grief and loneliness and that I've lost my ability to make wise choices."

Jim responded with scripture, "Woe to those who go down to Egypt for help and rely on horses, who trust in chariots and in the great strength of their horsemen, but do not look to the Holy One of Israel or consult the Lord" (Isa. 31:1). I replied, "Yes, Jim, I agree. This is saying woe to those who trust in man instead of trusting in God."

Jim became frustrated and said he was hanging up on me because he was about to cry. He went into a long prayer about the Lord teaching us to be kind in heart so that love, grace, and charity flow like a river. Requests for us to have hearts of generosity like Jesus, Our Lord, and to be like the rich young ruler and sell our possessions to give to the poor. He prayed for us to give freely without counting the cost and to let nothing in this world keep us from reflecting His generosity. On and on went the prayer. Does the Lord hear the prayers of sinners? Oh, I think he *hears* their prayers but according to John 9:31 (ESV): "We know that God does not *listen* to sinners, but if anyone is a worshiper of God and does his will, God listens to them." There is a difference between hearing and listening. Hearing is the reception of a sound, and listening is the receiving of the sound and really paying attention.

My text reply: "Dear Lord, I thank you for being love and giving us the feeling of love. I ask You to forgive me when I don't reflect Your light. Now I ask that you comfort Jim and help him to get rid of his frustration and to trust You in all things. Provide for his needs and give him the peace in his heart that comes only from You. Please lead both of us to have clarity and assurance. In Jesus' name, Amen."

Monday, December 19, 12:11 p.m.

The USPS inspector called and said not to expect to get any of the money back but that they were still tracking the mailings and investigating. He advised me to block Jim's number because he would just continue to harass me. I didn't block it, though. At this point, I was just curious to see where Jim would go next with his story!

Monday, December 19, 4:33 p.m.

Jim started the day by asking me to send $5,000 cash and mail it to the agent. I replied, "I don't have access to it." Jim said okay, that even $3,000 would help him make huge progress. I didn't answer right away, and he became agitated and said he was asking me a question; would I please answer him? I replied with a question: "Jim, do I pay my bills or yours? You know I would help you if I could. If I hadn't sent the $40,000, I wouldn't be in this mess with my kids. Could you get a loan using your car as collateral?" Of course, he said he had already done that and received $7,000 and only needed me to send the $3,000. I said, "I know you want me to pull a rabbit out of a hat, but I can't! I'll keep your Christmas presents tucked away until you get here." In anger, he told me to not worry about him that I was obviously putting my kids first. Then, he said, "*I give up!*"

Sunday, December 25, 1:12 p.m.

I didn't hear from Jim again until Christmas Day. In that message, he berated me for not texting to find out what was happening with him. He said he was dying. I thought, well that would be a great end to the story! Miraculously, two days later, he said his injury turned out to be a minor back issue caused from a fall on the platform. He was in Mexico and needed between $7,000 and $9,000 to pay his hospital bill and the flight to Knoxville. Like a broken record, I reminded him that I couldn't pay. He said okay; just send $1,650 for his ticket.

He continued to play his evil game. I thought about what the postal inspector had told me about blocking his number. It didn't appear that the FBI or the USPS would use my connection with him to track him down. I told myself I would block his number and put this all behind me, but I didn't.

Sunday, January 1, 5:50 a.m.

I sent Jim this text: "Please know that as the curtain closes on this play, that whoever you are and wherever you are, *you are loved*! God is pursuing you with the greatest love there is, ever has been, or ever will be! The Lord said, 'I will judge each of you for what you've done. So, stop sinning, or else you will certainly be punished. Give up your evil ways and start thinking pure thoughts. And be faithful to Me! Do you really want to be put to death for your sins? I, the Lord God, don't want to see that happen to anyone. So, stop sinning and live!' (Ezek. 18:30–32)."

Jim did not respond to this message. The months clicked by, and he did not reach back out again. Just maybe it really was over! Just maybe I will meet the real Jim in heaven some day!

IT'S BEEN SAID that without valleys, we wouldn't have mountaintops! Life is full of ups and downs, valleys, and mountaintops. During this twelve-month period, I had been in more than one valley, and I was reaching for the mountaintops!

I scraped and clawed my way back out of the valley. I had grieved the loss of my dear husband of forty-nine years, and I had grieved the loss of what I thought was my second chance at love. It was no small effort to share my failure with my family. I was devastated, ashamed, embarrassed, and an emotional wreck. I had that same feeling of walking around in a "fog" like I had experienced after David's death. I couldn't eat or sleep, and I could barely function. I told my family that I felt like a stupid idiot! They were all absolutely great, and loved and supported me through it.

As I reflected on all of this, I wondered what happened to me. Since David's death, I had been meditating on God's Word and praying more than ever. Did I not hear God's voice? Did I not wait upon Him or stay still long enough to hear Him? Or did I just want to have it my own way? My discernment and logical thinking had left me. My loneliness had led me there, and the void had been filled with longing and excitement. Yes, there would be times when I would question the realness of the situation, but I wouldn't let myself abandon the idea of a second chance at love. I didn't want to live out my days alone. I wrestled with God at the same time that I was trying to listen to His voice. I fought and struggled against Him to seek my own desires. "Temptation comes from our own desires, which entice us and drag us away" (Jim 1:14 NLT). Fortunately, God finally got my attention, and I clearly heard His voice!

Surprisingly, I wasn't all that upset about the $40,000 that I had given away. I was not financially wealthy. I hadn't even collected life insurance because it expired two months before David's death. In years past, we had money stolen from us, and we had lost money. Actually, it was a lot more money than I would want to admit. My classic statement has been, "It's just money!" Now, I must say I would prefer to make wiser decisions about how to spend the money God has entrusted to me. When I was in the Philippines the month before the scam began, I had considered giving $25,000 to build a church in David's memory. I wish I had!

After my final text to Jim, I knew that I wasn't even mad at him. I had no desire to seek prosecution or revenge.

God will judge us or reward us according to what we do. Remember Romans 12:19 (ESV): "Beloved, never avenge yourselves, but leave it to the wrath of God for it is written, 'Vengeance is mine, I will repay, says the Lord.'" As quickly as I had lost my peace, it returned. Praise to our Father!

I began preparing to face whatever valley God would allow me to slip into next. You may know the saying that we are coming out of a valley, we are in a valley, or getting ready to be in one! I'm just so thankful that I lived with the assurance that He will be with me through the dark valleys and restore the light again. I hold on to this scripture: "The sun will no more be your light by day, nor will the brightness of the moon shine on you, for the Lord will be your everlasting light, and your God will be your glory. Your sun will never set again, and your moon will wane no more; the Lord will be your everlasting light, and your days of sorrow will end" (Isa. 60:19–20 NIV).

I had found healing and peace that undeniably comes only through abiding in the Lord. I wasn't in the valley any longer, but brokenness leaves scars. I had scars on my ankle and scares on my heart. These scars would serve as reminders of things I had lived through and survived. These experiences would open up doors of understanding and compassion. God has used and will continue to use these life experiences as long as I live.

LIFE IS A journey, and unexpected things happen along the way. In December 2021, I had COVID, and twelve months later, December 2022, I had COVID again. Those episodes of COVID were the bookends for the events that crashed my world. My husband passed away; six months later, I broke my ankle and had surgery; ten months later, I spent the month of October in the Philippines; and months eleven and twelve, I succumbed to the evils of a scam. The only way I kept my head above water during these events was through the strength of the Lord. He used His Word and His people to support me and carry me.

I began to praise the Lord for emotional, physical, and spiritual healing. I considered that He left me here for reasons I needed to discover. I was beginning to find my new identity as a widow and as His child. I had begun to realize that *He is enough*! How thankful I had become for the days of confinement due to injury and then quarantine. It was during that time of quiet and reflection that I found time to pass through grief. God knew that if I had not been physically confined, I would not have stopped long enough to pass through these valleys. Without it, I wouldn't have felt the presence and comfort of the Lord nearly as intimately.

This also provided me with the motivation and time to record my valleys and struggles that I might share with others the amazing ways God works. His Word tells us that we don't just go through our trials and then we're done! No, we should anticipate more trials as we navigate through life. "So be truly glad. There is wonderful joy ahead, even though you must endure many trials for a little while. These trials will show that your faith is genuine. It is being tested as fire tests and purifies gold—though your faith is far more precious than mere gold. So, when your faith remains strong through many trials, it will bring you much praise and glory and honor on the day when Jesus Christ is revealed to the whole world" (1 Pet. 1:6–7 NLT). If we are wise enough to learn God's lessons in our trials, each valley should be easier to navigate because of the previous climbs.

From valley to valley and mountaintop to mountaintop, the Lord shows up to carry us through. He reveals more and more of His character, His ways, and His love. He is always there, and He never changes. As His children, we are the ones changing. We become more and more like Jesus when we schedule time to be in His presence, read and meditate on His Word, and converse with Him each day. No matter how mature we think we are in our spiritual walk and faith, the sin lurking about in this world will always challenge us. We must draw wisdom and strength from His Word in order to be prepared to stand up for truth and identify evil. The Word tells us we are in a spiritual battle and must fight until His return. We will most certainly slip and fall along our journey but walking *daily* with Him (not once in a while) will prevent us from *totally* slipping away. Whatever we would like to be found doing when Christ returns is exactly what we should be doing today. So, *we must devour the Word, pray like warriors, and witness like commissioned soldiers.* He's there for me and He's there for you; yesterday, today, and forever. Join me and let's reach out and seek His face. *We are only one breath away from eternity.*

Dear Lord, I want to see you! I want to feel Your very presence and savor You more fully. I pray that I will be ready in an instant to share You more freely. In Jesus' name, Amen.

Resources for Drawing Nearer to God

https://www.intouch.org Daily devotions and sermons

https://www.billygraham.org/Christian Daily devotions, topics, answers, and resources

You Version Bible app contains Bible reading plans, the entire Bible in numerous versions, videos, guided prayer, local events, and more

Bible Gateway Audio Bible, For times on the go.

https://www.thebiblerecap.com A one-year chronological plan for Bible reading with a five- to eight-minute summary and highlight of each day's reading. This podcast has kept me on track and interested in each day's reading.

Music is also beneficial in our drawing near to our Lord. I am enjoying "It Is Well With My Soul Radio", and "Maranatha Music Radio". I found these on Pandora.

These are just a few of the numerous resources available to assist you in your walk with God. Seek a local church and participate in small group activities with other Christians. We need fellow Christians to strengthen and build each other up. We need others in order to protect ourselves from the "evil one."

For those who are walking through loss and grief, seek out a Grief Share program at a local church. There you will find comfort in knowing you are not the only one navigating the waters of grief.

May the Lord bless you and keep you and make His face shine upon you.

The first Thanksgiving (2022) without Grandad became Hat Day. We all wore a hat, army jacket, or UT sweatshirt that had belonged to Grandad in his memory. Remembering how much David smiled and laughed, we thought this silly picture would have made him happy.

CPSIA information can be obtained
at www.ICGtesting.com
Printed in the USA
JSHW041050110723
44526JS00003B/6